D0904293

THE

SALES AUTOMATION

EVERYTHING YOU NEED TO KNOW, BEFORE YOU NEED TO KNOW IT

DICK LEE

Better Books

The Sales Automation Survival Guide—Everything you need to know, before you need to know it.

©1998 Richard A. Lee. All rights reserved.

No part of this book may be reproduced or transmitted in any form by any means, electronic or manual, including photocopying, recording or by any information storage and retrieval system without written permission from the author, except for the inclusion of brief quotations in a review.

Lee, Richard A.
    The Sales Automation Survival Guide: Everything you need to know, before you need to know it/Dick Lee

        p. cm.

Includes glossary

ISBN 1-886656-07-X

Library of Congress Catalog
Card Number: 96-78125

1. Sales automation   2. Sales force automation
3. Sales management 4. Computers—sales automation
5. Marketing   6. Selling   I. Title

Printed and bound in the United States of America.

02 01 00 99 98   10 9 8 7 6 5 4 3 2 1

THE
SALES AUTOMATION

SURVIVAL GUIDE

EVERYTHING YOU NEED TO KNOW,
BEFORE YOU NEED TO KNOW IT

TABLE OF CONTENTS

ACKNOWLEDGMENTS

Until you write a book, you have no idea how important acknowledgments are. That's because, by the time you finish, your family and friends are half-ready to either kill you or write you off as a babbling idiot who writes copy out loud at the dinner table…the movies…wherever. Never mind this pap about "patience," "support" and "love and understanding." They're ready to do terrible things to you! And that goes for your dear professional colleagues, as well. Those who spent the entire time you were writing just waiting by the phone for your call. "Mind reading this section over again, good buddy?"

Yeah, writing a book wears out a lot of people. And in many respects, it's easier on the person writing than on those watching the process, especially when yours truly has to rewrite everything six times before calling it the "first" draft. But I survived. Hope everyone else did, too.

Funny, didn't hear much of a response. "Are you guys still speaking to me?" Not until I promise never to write another book, eh?

Seriously, you can't write a book without ending up indebted to a lot of people—like many of my clients, present and past, with whom I've learned what works and what doesn't. Unfortunately, I can't name them. They don't want their competitors to know what's about to hit them, when sales automation comes into play (or after it comes into play, since so many "victims" of sales automation refuse to believe that customer information is the new competitive battleground). So I'll just say a big blanket "thank you."

Thanks also to the many professional colleagues who encouraged me (foolish of them) and fed me information. Particular thanks to organizational development guy Ralph Jacobson for helping me better grasp the underlying meaning of sales automation for an organization and its employees; to data-based research guy David Mangen, for sharing his years of experience doing data analysis without developing redundant data warehouses. And to sales automation reseller Steve Prange, who forced me to qualify my criticism of his profession by proving that "technologically astute reseller" is not an oxymoron.

Thanks also to my excellent editing/production team at Better Books: copy and style editor Kristine Ellis, proofer Kathie Anderson, cover designer Jody Majeres, and text layout and pre-press production manager Kristine Anderson. All talented yet extremely easy to work with—an uncommon combination in the creative trades.

And thanks especially to my wife, Kathy Sanders, and my five-year-old son, Gus. They cheerfully sacrificed an awful lot to let me go off on a toot and write this book. Fortunately, Gus reads books a lot faster than I write them. Otherwise, he might have gotten really bored waiting for me to show up and do stuff. And fortunately, my wonderful wife, who has her own demanding career, decided to take up knitting again. That's almost as obsessive as book writing. Just hope I haven't been replaced by a ball of yarn.

INTRODUCTION

Today, no marketing topic, aside from the Internet, is capturing more attention than sales automation. And perhaps no topic, including the Internet, is causing more confusion.

Some see sales automation as the new miracle drug that can cure the pernicious illness of sales and marketing inefficiency, which they perceive as sapping the strength of business enterprises. For others, sales automation has proved to be a relatively untested drug that was rushed to market before discovery of its powerful side effects, which cause many takers to suffer more than recover. Yet others view sales automation as a method of fundamentally changing human behavior. And this view is countered by the popular perception that sales automation is a software commodity, which is purchased and distributed to employees much like a new word processor, spreadsheet or graphics package. What a mix! Throughout this book, I'll reconcile these conflicting views, while thoroughly discounting the notion that sales automation is "software."

Another component of the widespread confusion is the term itself. What does "sales automation" mean? It doesn't help that sales automation is already a misnomer (but one that I'll use in the book nonetheless; that's what most people call it, and I don't want to create even more confusion). In rapid succession, sales automation has broken through its original sales boundaries to include first marketing, then customer service. Now it's beginning to infiltrate such powerful principalities as financial services, logistics and even information technologies (IT)—places where it's either not particularly welcome or subject to being "shot on sight."

But fueled by the inescapable logic that business enterprises must become centered on their customers, rather than remaining self-centered as is their wont, sales automation is crossing the moats and scaling the walls of management to get into these places and others.

So what is it, really?

Sales automation has too many faces for a simple dictionary definition, so here's a complex one of my making:

sales automation n. 1: introduction of information-based process management to sales and marketing. 2: customer information management capability at the point of customer contact. 3: a linking of all customer information in the enterprise into one information system, focused at the point of customer contact. 4: an information flow designed around the needs of the customer first, and the internal needs of the enterprise second. 5: a term used today to describe tomorrow's "relationship management system," which pushes the management of most customer information out to customer relationship managers. 6: a term used to describe the shift away from "corporate out" data flow and the move toward "customer in" data flow. 7: the movement that ended the era of corporate-centric customer information management. 8: the first step in the movement away from reliance on "what" data—that is, quantitative information about customers' historical behavior—toward "why" data, the combination of qualitative and quantitative information that produces *customer knowledge.*

I could go on for another page, at least. A better use of that space (and your time) is to list the litany of labels associated with sales automation, labels you may be more accustomed to using.

- *Sales force automation* (SFA). The original nomenclature, this label expresses the initial, tight focus on automating field sales representatives.

- *Relationship management* (RM). This emerging term reflects the new focus on proactively managing customer relationships with the support of customer information that is integrated and accessible from every nook and cranny of the enterprise.

- *One-to-one marketing.* This wonderful term was coined by authors Don Peppers and Martha Rogers, whose books have elevated the importance of the customer in the mindset of many business organizations.[1] One-to-one marketing is a principal outcome of sales automation, but not the only outcome.

- *Customer information management* (CIM). CIM is the process of managing customer information in support of selling and relationship management.

- *Customer information system* (CIS). CIS is the systems portion of CIM (although I must hasten to add that CIS is also used to describe a common tragedy called the "marketing data warehouse," which I'll lament more than once as we progress).[2]

- *Customer knowledge management.* This refers to what I call the progression from current reliance on "what" data to a future melding of qualitative and quantitative information about customers to produce customer knowledge—the "why" data. You won't hear the term "customer knowledge management"

---

[1] Don Peppers and Martha Rogers, *The One to One Future; Building Relationships One Customer at a Time* (New York: Doubleday, 1993); *Enterprise One To One,* (New York: Doubleday, 1997).

[2] I'm deliberately misusing the term "tragedy," defined by classic Greek civilization as taking place over a 24-hour time period. Marketing data warehouses unfold over years. But you could fill a coliseum with all the consultants a single data warehouse consumes.

on the street today, but with the rush to share more than "hard data" in the engineering and operations business sectors, it's only a matter of time.

That's enough. You get the picture. And whatever your expectations of this book, you certainly know by now whether you're in the right church. The right pew? Don't worry about it, because the book might influence you to "change pews," perhaps more than once. And if you're after information about building a customer data warehouse, I hope you read on despite my snide remarks. I'll give you several compelling reasons *not* to build one, at least not in this context, which could save you lots of time, trouble and money. Besides, I don't disapprove of all data warehouses. Just the ones built at the wrong time for the wrong reasons.

Having said all that, let me add what this book is not about. This book is not about being a shill for sales automation and the sales automation industry. Yes, it's true that in almost every organization where individual customers have appreciable lifetime value, sales automation is rising to the top of the agenda. And it's still in its early adolescence, with years of explosive growth ahead.

But sales automation is also an "adolescent" with a troubled past.

You need to know about this, too. From the get-go, sales automation promised huge gains in customer lifetime value as well as greatly diminished customer churn. It also promised to cure the "inherent inefficiency" of the sales process (often described as the lack of sales process). Hey, if sales automation can help us more effectively acquire and manage contact-level customer information, and help us use that information to cash in on more customer development opportunities, and keep our customers around longer so we don't have to spend lots on marketing to replace them, and even encourage more productivity from field sales representatives (those folks who deserve to be burned at the stake for filling the trunks of their company cars with golf clubs, fishing tackle and other gear to play with while everyone else is working)—if sales automation can accomplish all this, how can we go wrong?

And in some cases, sales automation has gone very right. To quote the Harvard Business Review :

> "Sales increases arising from advanced marketing and sales technology have ranged from 10% to more than 30%, and investment returns have often exceeded 100%. These returns may sound like the proverbial free lunch, but they are real."[3]

But that's far from the whole story. Let's balance this message of success with an adult dose of reality supplied by several parties closer to the action on a day-by-day basis.

Sales process trainer Barry Trailer, one of the senior members of the sales automation movement, writes,

> "It's been proven that [sales automation] projects can get off the ground. However, more are crashing than flying, and even those that stay aloft seem unstable much of the time."[4]

The Gartner Group, highly respected technology markets researchers and consultants, studied its own clients and found that 60% of top-performing sales reps wouldn't use sales automation—and didn't appear to be suffering for it.[5] Similar depressing numbers abound. Not exactly an unbridled success we have going here.

---

[3] Rowland T. Moriarty and Gordon S. Swartz, "Automation to Boost Sales and Marketing." *Harvard Business Review* (January-February 1989).

[4] Barry Trailer, "Can We Talk," *Sales & Field Force Automation*, July 1997

[5] Ken Delaney, "The Automated Sales Force," *Marketing Tools*, (October 1996) pp. 57-63.

From a pavement-level perspective, sales automation usually does produce more pain than gain. And while there's plenty of blame to spread around for this, *nothing leads to more pain than treating sales automation as a software purchase*—a mistake that occurs in a majority of first-time sales automation implementations and that recurs in those organizations immune to learning from past experience.

Here's the drill. Some "speed is life" manager trucks on down to Software R Us; buys a few gross of Acme Software's "Sell Your Brains Out (or we'll have the data we need to fire your butt"); and then ships it to all the reps with a memo saying, "Use it."

"And by the way," the P.S. on the memo instructs, "if you don't have a laptop, buy yourself one. It's your responsibility to come to work properly equipped."

You probably think I'm exaggerating.

Unfortunately, I'm not. And what happens next? Mr. Speed Is Life blames his failure on the software and on the hapless souls on the receiving end of this folly—and then does it all over again with a bigger and better software program. Sort of like shooting yourself in the foot with a pistol, then picking up an AK-47 to do it right.

The first rule of successful sales automation is:

Sales automation is not software.

Rather, it's a fundamental change in sales and marketing processes, including human behavior, accompanied by a significant domino effect that will reach into the far corners of the organization. Because organizations take sales automation so lightly, the pain that inevitably accompanies *any* functional re-engineering comes as a shock. So much so that the first sign of organizational pain often stops sales automation dead in its tracks. "No one told us this was going to happen." "Yeah, it's important, but we can't afford to tick off so and so." And, "Hey, why torture ourselves over a piece of software?"

You can imagine what hits the fan when an executive VP in charge of all information technology discovers that some less-than-executive VP of sales and marketing is running a competitive information system using mail-order laptops and some strange hybrid of process management and database software. Or when the executive VP of operations discovers that his or her reports in district management are being asked to have district salespeople pipe volumes of district-level customer information back to some John or Jane Doe marketing analyst.

Most sales automation industry pundits estimate the incidence of failure to achieve primary sales automation objectives at 50% to 75%, and that's just systems that get off the drawing board. From what I've experienced wading through the wreckage left by failed or partially installed, never-finished pro-jects, 75% is more like it. If we include sales automation ini-tiatives that die or go on permanent hold during the preliminary discussion stage, that figure would rise yet higher.

MISTAKING SALES AUTOMATION FOR SOFTWARE IS USUALLY A FATAL ERROR

Obviously, there's a problem. The temptation of tremen-dous gains in sales and marketing productivity is hanging out there like the proverbial carrot—and most who reach for those gains are getting whacked with the proverbial stick.

Why?

Answering the "why" question for potential victims was the primary purpose for writing this book. I'll take a close look at what's behind sales automation failures to make sure you're forewarned and forearmed.

But I'm not going to dwell on failure. Instead, I want to focus on overcoming the obstacles that trip up so many sales automation programs, and then move along and look at how and where sales automation really can be worth the risk and effort.

Whether you're in sales, marketing, customer service, information technology, operations or corporate management, reading this book should greatly increase the odds that you'll be ready to do your part in the complex process of implementing sales automation in your organization. And the book will also take you one step further.

Technology limitations, such as the difficulty in getting different databases to communicate with each other, still limit sales automation's progression beyond the boundaries of sales, marketing and sometimes customer service. Fortunately, forward-thinking software developers, often pushed by forward-thinking sales automation users, are gradually overcoming these limitations.

The net of their efforts will be *enterprise sales automation*—a future where sales automation systems will extend from the point of customer contact right into the bowels of corporate information systems, encompassing every piece of information pertaining to each individual customer (and what we're likely to call "customer knowledge management" in the future). You're about to get a firsthand look at enterprise sales automation through real work in process—a sneak preview of where the sales automation phenomenon is headed, and where you just might want to head yourself.

Three quick notes before we start. First, about the cases described in the book. I have a responsibility to my clients not to let competitors know what they're up to. So do the consultants and sales automation software suppliers who shared their stories with me. Consequently, I've disguised all of the cases and even blended several to discourage guessing. So don't guess. It won't do you any good to know.

Second, about my seeming favoritism toward salespeople throughout the book. I'm not an apologist for the sales profession.

In fact, I take a dim view of the profession's all-too-common resistance to process improvement, technology and almost any form of change. Yet, from the sales side of the fence, I also understand how much of sales' "negative" behavior is giving back what they get. I also know that sales automation is virtually impossible to implement in an environment where attitudes such as "getting back at sales" or "teaching sales a lesson" or "bringing sales to heel" are mixed in with sales automation.

Before implementing sales automation, we all need to swallow hard and exorcise whatever rancor we hold toward any sales automation participants. And if we have a hard time doing so with regard to sales, try looking in the mirror and asking why we're not jumping at the opportunity to "earn their money" and "enjoy goofing off on the job." Heck, virtually every one of my clients asks me for help finding good salespeople. There's a job waiting for you out there—if you enjoy burnout, love rejection and thrive on living with uncertainty. Not to mention the enjoyment of being dumped on by everyone who envies your pay and your "freedom" but doesn't have a clue about the price you pay, nor a willingness to pay it if they did.

Think I'm pushing a point too far? Take it from another source. Here's what Eugene Johnson, marketing professor and co-author of the recent study "Attitudes of College Students Towards Selling" has to say. "They [college students] believe there is money to be made in sales, but they often don't want to do the necessary things to make that money."[6]

And third, about the tenor of the book. You've already had a taste of my sarcasm. I assure you, it will only get worse. I considered toning it down. But every time that thought arose, so did the image of a delicious quote from Freud, which I saw posted outside a client's office door.

---

[6] Andy Cohen, "Sales Strikes Out on Campus," *Sales and Marketing Management* (November 1997).

Insanity
Doing the same thing over and over again,
but expecting a different outcome.

That's an apt description of sales automation today. We keep trying. Most of us keep failing. And we keep on making the same damn mistakes, over and over again. The time has passed for a polite tome about this or that aspect of sales automation. It's time to start getting in people's faces about this stuff.

Besides, on a personal level, it's getting really hard to watch it happen over and over again. So please forgive a periodic acid tongue.

Dick Lee
High-Yield Marketing
dleehym@ix.netcom.com

I.
UNDERSTANDING
SALES
AUTOMATION

THE INSIDE STORY

SALES AUTOMATION-SPEAK

A number of confusing and overlapping terms related to sales automation have already worked their way into our sales and marketing lexicon. Consciously or unconsciously, we're going to be using a number of these terms before we finish. So better to clarify them now than later, including several of the labels I described briefly in the Introduction. (If, later on, you again become confused, check the Glossary of Acronyms and Other Potentially Befuddling Terms at the end of this book for quick clarification.)

Sales Automation

"Sales automation" is an umbrella term describing the planned and coordinated use of network, desktop, laptop and even palm-top computers that are linked by specialized software to manage sales, marketing and customer service activities. It's computer-driven *process management* that breaks down sales, marketing and service functions into discrete steps, and then manages and measures each step.

That's a far cry from managing your personal calendar with store-bought software; or from "getting fancy" and buying software that tells you when to send follow-up letters and when to follow up on your letters by telephone (and tells management whether you've carried out these steps); or from linking your marketing database to e-mail so every man, woman and child at corporate can download, direct to the field, thousands of unqualified "prospect" names and millions of extraneous e-mail messages.

As it is commonly used, the term "sales automation" is often bastardized to include anything involving a computer, "sales automation" software, customer names and your personal calendar. But it's not the real deal unless it is (a) *planned* to improve customer relationship management (as opposed to just sales rep calendar management); (b) *coordinated* to share customer and market information among different users and different levels of users; and (c) process-related, permitting continuous improvement of all processes involving direct and indirect interaction with customers.

SALES AUTOMATION DATA COMES PRIMARILY FROM THE POINT OF CUSTOMER CONTACT. ALL OTHER DATA SOURCES ARE SECONDARY.

And we can't leave out one more important aspect of sales automation—*it's anchored by customer data captured at the point of customer contact*. Not data captured in corporate accounting, not data stored in a central direct marketing database (nor, ugh, a customer data warehouse that collects everything except information captured directly from customers), not credit bureau data, not third-party data from departments of motor vehicles or mailing-list compilers or trade associations or trade publications. I mean data captured direct from the horse's mouth, so to speak. And that's what makes sales automation data more accurate, more powerful and more actionable than any other source of customer information.

Enterprise Sales Automation

Enterprise sales automation is a natural outgrowth of automating sales, service and marketing functions. Having gone that far, the next step is seeing the potential of going further. Fully implemented, enterprise sales automation incorporates the customer-specific financial and operations data that are normally kept locked away in corporate vaults, where "loose cannons" like us sales and marketing types can't mess with it. It ties together everything the organization knows about the customer, and offers the opportunity to know more by providing a "home" for customer intelligence and information of innumerable types.

Enterprise sales automation provides the binoculars that enable customer-contact types to see deep into those corporate data vaults. It even organizes all this "hidden" data so that customer-contact people can see what they need to see without searching hither, thither and yon. As if that wasn't enough, enterprise sales automation also provides a pipeline for front-line folks to ship significant customer data to management and to staff types, and to receive data back (although much less than most corporate types are inclined to send them).

However, opening up this two-way flow of data tends to upset many gatekeepers of corporate data—especially those accustomed to tightly controlling what leaves their data vaults, and even worse, what enters. The need-not-to-know is a surprisingly powerful force in many organizations. But we'll talk about all these hindrances to implementing enterprise sales automation later.

BASIC ENTERPRISE SALES AUTOMATION

Operations	Management	Financial

Marketing	Sales	Service

Customer

Just as sales automation is centered on customer information, enterprise sales automation is centered on the total relationship management needs of the sales and service functions, with a secondary focus on marketing's information and communication needs. Even though enterprise sales automation actively supports functions that operate at a distance from customers—accounting, inventory control, logistics, product development, human resources and others—its focus must be on relationship management needs. There are two reasons for this. First, because customer-direct data, which makes the wheels of sales automation turn, is mined by customer relationship managers in sales and service. And second, because successful implementation of sales automation, to any degree, requires a high-level of compliance from relationship managers, which in the case of sales, is often given grudgingly.

Relationship managers have to mine the data. They have to use it. And history shows that *only* sales automation programs designed around their needs ever succeed in winning their cooperation. It's that simple. Never let anyone in any position of power persuade you that they can *order* relationship managers to dutifully use a sales automation system. Hasn't happened yet. Probably never will.

> **EXTRACTING CUSTOMER INFORMATION CAN BE HARD WORK. RELATIONSHIP MANAGERS WON'T DO IT UNLESS IT'S IN THEIR BEST INTEREST.**

Remote Data Synchronization

It's hard to talk about sales automation software without first discussing remote data synchronization—unless all of your sales automation users happen to sit linked to one network, in which case you can skip this section until you get a new job elsewhere.

Development of data synchronization technology contributed almost as much to the precipitous rise of sales automation as did the advent of laptop computers. But it's a good bet that you know a lot more about laptop computers than about some quirky deal called "remote data synchronization," *n'est pas?* And that's why we're really going to get into this subject and roll around in it for a while.

It's hard to talk about remote data synchronization without confusing the daylights out of non-technical people. Or boring the plastic-pocket-liner contingent half-to-death. But I'll try to find a happy medium, or at least a mutually unhappy medium. This is "gotta know" territory, unless you're all happily camped around a central computer network.

Data synchronization is a fancy term for the simultaneous exchange of new or changed data among non-networked computers (which ain't too shabby an expression itself). Let's try that again. Data synchronization means swapping data between non-networked computers in order to keep everyone running on the same data.

Fortunately for this discussion (but not for enterprise sales automation folks like myself), with few exceptions, current technology limits synchronization to exchanges of data among computers running the same sales automation software programs. In other words, at the time of this writing you can't synchronize GoldMine with Maximizer. Nor can you synchronize data between more sophisticated sales automation software such as Saratoga Systems' Avenue or Optima's Teamworks.

While this barrier is crumbling around the edges and will fall sometime in the foreseeable future, for now we'll ignore the topic of moving data back and forth among different software programs. No sense getting knee-deep in techno-babble until you get your feet wet with sales automation.

To sum it up, remote data synchronization permits multiple users who run the same sales automation software on their computers, but who are *not* permanently linked to each other via a network, to exchange data so everyone has the latest and greatest information.

And how, pray tell, does this miracle called "synchronization" actually occur?

Here's how. The synchronization of more than two computers relies on two elements:

1. *A reference database* of true facts, or at least the latest facts, housed on a central computer. Sales automation types often refer to this central computer as "the server." (Although it's not a true server in IT-speak). After all, when you're networked to a central

server and everyone is sharing one database, there's
no need to synchronize.)

2. *Communication links* established from the sales
   automation server to remote users.

When that server is at corporate HQ and all the remote
users dutifully synchronize directly with the server, that's:

One-step, or WAN (for "wide area network"), synchronization.
Remote users temporarily connect to the WAN to synchronize,
then leave the network until the next time they synchronize.
Simpler than it sounds.

If there's "one-step" synchronization, you're probably guessing that "two-step" synchronization comes next. Unfortunately,
especially if you're reading this book in bed and trying to stay
awake, you're right. We're going to have to discuss it.

Two-step, or LAN (for "local area network"), synchronization. In
two-step synchronization, individual remote users synchronize
with a field server housed at their local or regional office. That
server, in turn, synchronizes with the central server. Simple
again, except for one wrinkle.

Most two-step synchronization systems never get past step
one. That's because sales automation grew out of field salespeople deciding they wanted to share information locked away on
their laptops or desktops. So they would all troop down to
Software R Us and buy the same software program, put it on
their expense accounts, and then eagerly load it and try
exchanging data. Crash!...crash!...crash!...crash!

So much for step one. Unless they got very lucky in their
software selection, they regretted wanting to communicate
with each other. Most store-bought, canned software doesn't
synchronize well. Nor, for that matter, does it network well, if
at all. Still, these brave sales automation pioneers persevered
and patched things together as best they could. But after their
travails, few even attempted the second step: forging the link to

corporate HQ and through corporate to other field offices. And in truth, many were happy *not* to share anything with corporate. "The less those bozos know the better."

Most two-step sales automation systems remain in this state today. Worse yet, many organizations have different offices running different sales automation software programs that can't synchronize with each other. *Until organizations set and support uniform sales automation software standards that permit synchronization, there will be no sales automation.* Autonomy-loving relationship managers love this situation. At least they think they do. Until they lose that huge, multi-product-line customer to a competitor whose sales and service reps in different product lines can communicate, coordinate and cooperate to the delight of their customers.

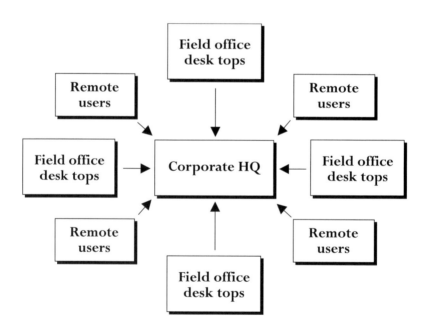

WAN-sync (one-step synchronization),
all data passes through a single hub.

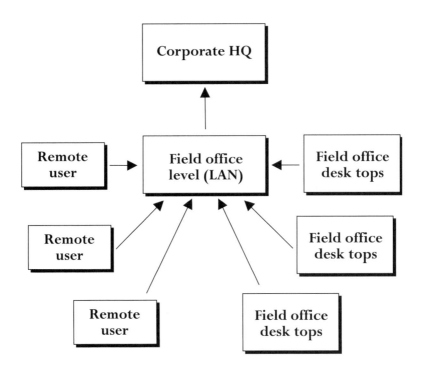

With LAN-sync (two-step synchronization), data synchronization occurs at both regional and enterprise levels.

Enough about "one-step, two-step" stuff. To avoid confusion, let's just use "WAN-sync" for one-step and "LAN-sync" for two-step. *Simplement.*

Okay. We've got a head of steam going. On to the next matter.

Aside from choosing between WAN-sync and LAN-sync, you also have to select among several different methods of communicating among computers. Originally, a plain old modem connection over standard telephone lines was the connection of choice. Dial up the central computer. Synchronize. Disconnect. See you later. You pay the phone bill. The only real alternative back then was "sneaker-net" synchronization, which, thankfully, has pretty much run its course.

Sneaker-net synchronization was about as ineffective as it was informal. Friday morning sales meeting at the regional office: "Let's swap disks and update while we're waiting for Brock and Nancy to show up."

"Hey Charley, wipe the damn jelly off your fingers before you handle my diskette."

"Mary, watch your blankety-blank coffee, you're spilling it on my laptop."

"Hey, let's think about getting one o' them virus protection programs, since we're all running each other's disks every week. And Brock told me he downloads stuff off the Internet."

"Never mind Brock. This is about your kid coming home from college next week."

"Hey, if we buy one, we can all share it."

"That's illegal.

"So what."

That's sneaker net. I've even worked with clients whose national account reps were mailing diskettes back and forth across the country to each other. That's dedication. Or was it desperation?

Keeping up with the times, Internet synchronization through a Web-based central database has become the snazzy way to go, especially for WAN-sync. Sort of alliterative. *"Web-sync,WAN-sync."* Cool stuff. Synchronizing by sending data update files through corporate e-mail systems over high-speed phone lines is also catching on in both WAN and LAN environments. Pretty mundane. Half cool and half mundane is the hybrid method of using Internet e-mail to exchange update files.

Okay, we're done with synchronization, at least the technical side. No more tech talk for now. But we're not quite done with the Internet and its appropriate role (or non-role) in synchronization. You may have noticed, the "I" word appear not once, but twice, in that last paragraph. And the "W" word came up once. Make you wonder whether I'm a victim of the "incredible trendiness of Net?"

No way. I didn't say *I favored* synchronizing over the Net (might as well use the "N" word, too). Just that organizations are doing it. That's fine if you have a "private line," but not if you have to rely on a "party line" supplied by a commercial Internet service provider (ISP for lovers of techie-terms). For example, If you were an American Online (AOL) subscriber during its flat-rate marketing fiasco in late 1996 - early 1997, you're probably not synchronizing over a party line anymore, for reasons that should make us all shy away from trusting the Internet for synchronization.

The AOL debacle, along with a myriad of smaller scale Internet "outages" are becoming a fact of everyday life. (In fact, rather than standing for "Internet service provider," "ISP" now stands for "intermittent service provider.") That raises serious issues. Can you rely on an ISP now? Will things be better or worse three years from now? The smart money is on "worse."

> **WHEN IT COMES TO DATA SYNCHRONIZATION, THE INTERNET IS AN UNRELIABLE PARTNER.**

Yeah, the Internet's fun, it's sexy, it's chic and—and it's damn dangerous, unless you own your own piece of it. Think about the poor sales rep who hasn't been able to synchronize for a day and a half and who walks in on his company's best customer, unaware that Accounts Receivable is dunning them on a bill that has now been paid twice, for equipment that didn't work when they first got it and just broke down again yesterday (parts will be available in two weeks)…"Hi! What a gorgeous day!" Blam.

Remember those golf clubs? The fishing rod? Go through that scenario a couple times in one day and you'd flee to the course or the lake for the rest of the week.

But with sales automation on the job, sales has to stay on the job. Big Brother is watching. And if we're going to deny sales the "mental health" benefits they earn by going through scenes like this, scenes that would make most of us turn tail and run (especially after the third one of the morning), we have to give them something in return. Prominent among "things in return" should be a *reliable early-warning system*, so that relationship managers can manage these situations rather than get mangled by them. Unless, of course, we don't really want to give sales anything; we just want to get back at them for their evil ways. In which case we'll wind up with lots of disgruntled relationship managers jumping ship and heading for saner shores—with lots of our best customers in tow.

Sort of like ships leaving a sinking rat.

For the benefit of readers who have never "carried the bag" (been in sales), I'll use my own experience as a sales rep to illustrate how this new *quid pro quo* with relationship managers must work. Must work, that is, if you want to keep your good customer relationship managers, and in many cases your good customers.

I was in Boston working for a national bus company, where I was part of a brazen attempt to compete with Federal Express, Airborne Express and others in the small package, overnight delivery business. We had lots of empty space underneath the busses; the busses were already running; we could hire independent courier companies to pick up and deliver. Easy pickin's, no?

Not too long before I joined the company, some marketing genius decided that BusCo should accept every package it could lay its hands on during a mother of a national United Parcel Service strike, in 1978. Yeah, and fit 'em all under the busses. People whose packages we carried—and almost inevitably lost, damaged or delayed—were not happy campers. Nor, for that matter, were the passengers whose luggage we lost in the process.

Everyone talks about how rough New York is, but I've worked in both New York and Boston, and Boston back then was much meaner. I'd cold call shippers in Boston's garment district and tell them I was from BusCo: "You know, the guys with the terminal you wouldn't dare visit after dark." Some wouldn't believe we'd carry freight—cuz, heck, even our packages could get mugged. Others saw no humor whatsoever in our presence.

I'd see a snarl start at the guy's mouth and gradually spread until his face was so contorted they should have slapped a latex mold on him and made Halloween masks. Then he'd start moving his hand toward the drawer of his metal shipping desk. I'd edge towards the door. He'd jerk the drawer open and...whew, it was only a knife. I could still run back then.

What I didn't know, for want of sales automation, was that he was a customer, although definitely in the past tense. And he had entrusted his company's entire spring sample line to BusCo for shipment to New York for a fashion show. It was just nonstop between two terminals. But this was during the UPS strike. And we lost it. And this poor slob was ready to kill...me. And I didn't have a clue when I walked in the door. Nor, without real-time data through data synchronization, would I have known at the time we committed this heinous deed that we'd lost a critical shipment for a potentially high-volume customer. If a warning flag had appeared on the screen when I fired up my computer, I could have interceded with operations and begged for a special intervention (otherwise known as "looking for it") by the dock crew in New York.

So what did I do, after putting my life in peril because I knew squat about this customer's history? The same thing I always did when my conscience won out and I couldn't represent this jerry-built freight service with a straight face. I drove down to the fishing pier in South Boston, pulled out my always-present surf-casting rod (two-piece, so it fit into the trunk), bought some clams at the little concession at the foot of the pier and went flounder fishing. Not even a laptop to lock in the trunk.

My boss, an Irish sort named Peter Meehan who was sentenced to the New York office, later explained to me that the New York Port Authority terminal was so flooded with packages during this debacle that the loading crews started throwing them on any bus going anywhere, just to get them off the dock. They were still finding them long after I left the company for a safer job. Peter knew the score. When customer service in New York wouldn't answer the phones, usually because they were out on the dock racing forklifts, I'd call him and ask him to physically go down to the Port and look for a missing package shipped by a good customer. It might be on the dock, or in a bus that was grounded for maintenance, which most of ours were. I'd call him back, maybe about 6:30 or 7:00 p.m. to ask if he'd had any luck.

One time he answered, "Here's the good news, I found it."

Now here's the bad news. "It was under the bus."

To which I answered something like, "Well that's were it's supposed to be, or supposed to have *been*."

"No, you don't get it. It was under the wheels."

Then he switched the subject, "Let's talk about the important stuff. Did you catch anything?"

Hey, he knew. He also knew that I was more than making my numbers in a very difficult situation, and that he

OFTEN, AND FOR GOOD REASON, SALES REPS VIEW LAPTOPS AS "VIDEO MONITORS" THAT RECORD AND TRANSMIT THEIR EVERY MOVE.

had to cut me some slack to keep me on board. Even companies like Xerox encouraged their reps to go to the movies rather than make a bad call because they were still smarting from getting dented by an irate customer. And at BusCo, I took enough lumps to justify fishing morning, noon and night.

Time to dust yourself off, make sure your limbs are all intact, take your head out of the sling, restore your self-confidence and your confidence in what you're selling—sales automation takes all that away. You can't exactly enter "4 flounder, 1 skate, 2 sea robins" for your call results. You don't fake calls either, at least not for long before it or "they" catch up to you.

Sales automation taketh away some important sources of sanity from sales reps. And it also giveth some sanity back. Like synchronized, real-time data so that you know when to duck, and even more importantly, when to intercede to save a valuable customer relationship threatened by a miscue or misdeed or by some lippy, wet-behind-the-ears accounts receivable clerk filling up a daily quota of "situations brought to a head." Sales can't save themselves or their carefully nurtured relationships without *real-time data*. And sorry, but *the Internet is only real-time part of the time.* And that ain't good enough.

The sales automation system designers who get ectoplasmic over using the Internet are doing it to satisfy themselves, not to meet sales force needs. Sure we need to use the Internet to hang out product information, promotional tools, parts and price lists that sales can download. But that's not time-sensitive. Reps can wait for that stuff, or pull it down over the weekend when Web traffic slows down. But often you can't wait to synchronize.

Not to bash the Internet or anything like that, but there's another issue to discuss involving the deadly duo, Web-sync, WAN-sync. Don't try this combination with independent distributors.

It's hard enough to get your own company reps to share their customer data. Persuading independent distributors and distributor reps to synchronize data is much more difficult. And it becomes impossible when you tell them that you're going to take data from *their* laptops; beam it off some satellite back to *your* HQ (where you can steal it); then update each of *their* rep's data with data from *their* colleagues sitting ten feet away from them; and finally beam it all back via another satellite. If you're lucky, they'll laugh.

If you're going to partner with independent distribution on a sales automation system, better plan to use LAN-sync. That allows distributors to filter out data they don't want you to see—data that's probably none of your business, anyway.

Not to beat a dead horse, but several more problems weigh against using Web-sync, WAN-sync versus more earthly modes of synchronization.

- Slow Internet transmission speed wastes time.

- Temptation abounds for field staff to waste even more time by uploading everything but the kitchen sink.

- Temptation also abounds to dump every scrap of data the field people wasted so much time uploading into a marketing data warehouse, which will waste even more of everybody's time (more on that later).

Okay. Horse dead. Point made.

In the future, wireless data synchronization over cellular or "personal digital assistant" (PDA) devices will become a popular synchronization medium, particularly among high-tech field service technicians who need to travel light, move fast and have a full service history on screen before they arrive at their next location. But the data integrity of wireless telephone transfer is still shaky, and it may take years for our wireless telephone industry to agree on one, universal data transmission protocol, a feat the rest of the world quietly accomplished years ago. Unfortunately, bitter competition among U.S. wireless companies has kept uniform standards from washing up on our shores. The situation is ludicrous enough to wish for Bill Gates to step in and create a standard.

So much for synchronization. But don't breath a huge sigh of relief and forget about it. How you synchronize often determines how well critical user groups, such as sales, will accept and use your sales automation system. It's often a "make or break" decision in the sales automation design process.

Sales Automation Software

Although sales automation is not a software program, software programs are primary implementation tools. While choosing the "right" software doesn't come close to ensuring success, choosing the wrong software pretty much guarantees failure.

When we say "sales force automation software," we're referring to one or more of four different categories

THE FAILURE OF THE CELLULAR INDUSTRY TO AGREE ON A COMMON WIRELESS TRANSMISSION PROTOCOL LIMITS THE UTILITY OF CELLULAR AND DIGITAL DATA TRANSMISSION FOR SALES AUTOMATION.

of software. Unfortunately, only one of these four categories actually supports sales automation; but we'll cover all four because you'll need to know what's not good to use.

But remember as you read on: these are my opinions, based on what's in front of my nose at the time I'm writing this. Things change. Especially in the sales automation biz. So always be willing to hear folks out about what they've changed and improved.

Personal Information Managers (PIMs)

Now a mature software category, PIMs first appeared in the early 1980s when PCs arrived on the market. They started as electronic telephone books, then added auto-dialing through modems as modems became commonplace. Second-generation PIMs added personal calendars and more facilities for storing customer information, including searchable fields that enable us to call up lists of customers that meet the criteria we specify. We can even print labels, personalized letters and envelopes with upscale PIMs. Zippy. But not too zippy.

PIMs do great managing telephone numbers and calendars. For sales automation, they don't cut it. That's because they store static information, with few or no facilities for tracking activities, measuring outcomes or providing anything beyond very crude customer opportunity management.

PIMS REPLACE DESK DIRECTORIES AND APPOINTMENT BOOKS, BUT THEY AREN'T SALES AUTOMATION TOOLS.

Despite PIMs' limitations, the success of PDAs has given them a brief renaissance. PDAs lack sufficient memory and processing power to drive anything more robust. But their revival will last only as long as it takes to "bulk them up" without bulking them up, if you catch my drift. Already, PDAs have sufficient power to run "thin" versions of Windows 95. Before long, they'll run fully-featured sales automation software, ending the brief resurgence of the lowly PIM.

No matter how lowly, you should still know what's out there, if only FYI. Microsoft® Outlook, a big improvement over its predecessor, Schedule+, should soon dominate the PIM market. Warts and all. Because nothing else can touch it for integration with Microsoft Office. And because nothing can or will touch Microsoft Office for market share. And because Bill Gates has promised he'll fix problems like poor e-mail integration. (Or better yet, he'll make someone else fix them.)

Other popular PIMs that should survive the Outlook onslaught include Ecco Pro and Sidekick.

Oh yeah. One more word of caution about this whole category. In general, you're better off not trying to run PIMs over a "peer-to-peer" (no server) Windows 95 network. Even Outlook won't run over a Windows 95 network; it requires an expensive Microsoft Exchange Server. So, if you're going to run over any type of network, plan to spend the extra dollars for heavier-duty software.

Individual Contact Managers (ICMs)

One step above PIMs are individual contact managers, or ICMs. Their primary advantages are that they link the calendar to the customer database, allowing users to maintain contact histories as well as to more quickly set appointments from the basic contact screen; plus, they offer much more flexibility and range in storing customer data. Nothing to write home about, though.

Are they adequate for sales automation use? In my opinion, definitely not. In fact, I disrespectfully view them as placebos that individuals and organizations take when they don't want to bother with real sales automation.

The "individual" in individual contact manager says it all. Fine for individual use. But ICMs fail the most basic requirement of sales automation—sharing information with other relationship management stations. They're information islands unto themselves. Better to stay away from this software category entirely, lest salespeople get too comfortable with not sharing data.

Now here's the kicker. Although ICMs are a dead end for sales automation, a well-known software package from this category, ACT! from Symantec®, remains the sales leader for the entire "sales automation" software category.

Now what's wrong with this picture?

ACT! does claim that it's latest version (V3.0) will synchronize data among different users, and run over networks, too. I've never tried it, because ACT!'s lack of either a fully relational database or process management capabilities rule it out for the type work I do with my clients. But when I give presentations, especially when small-business people are present, I'm almost certain to be asked questions about ACT!

"Do you ever recommend it?"

"What do you think of it?"

Because I don't use it, I turn that question around and ask, "What do you think of it?" What I most commonly hear back are tales of woe about crashes during synchronization and networking issues, even with the latest version. ACT! and other ICMs like Sales Rep Pro and Janna Contact are usually adequate for an individual user with no plans to exchange data with anyone else and no need for relational databases. But not for sales automation software. Not ever, in my opinion.

Although the sales automation industry still has the youthful earnestness and sense of mission that prevents it from laughing at itself, Barry Trailer, whom I quoted earlier, got off quite a zinger during his presentation at a recent sales automation trade show. He asked his audience if they knew why ACT! is so popular with salespeople. After many expectant giggles from the audience, he answered his rhetorical question. "Because salespeople know that with ACT!, they won't have to share their customer information."

The roar of laughter from the audience reflected more than a little bit of "been there, done that." But the joke isn't on ACT! It's on all of the organizations that continue to use it or other ICMs for sales automation, despite the experiences of those who've already driven into that ditch.

ACT! and other ICMs have helped many individual sales reps become very successful sales reps. And ACT! in particular is marvelously easy to use. But hey, let's reserve ICMs for the right purpose—*individual* contact management.

Group Contact Managers (GCMs)

Several links higher on the sales automation software food chain are retail-sold contact management programs designed from inception to synchronize data among laptop or desktop computers as well as to run over networks. Leading GCM players are GoldMine, Maximizer and TeleMagic (the latter used primarily by telemarketers). A notable new entry is a combination of ACT! and Lotus Notes, marketed primarily by IBM® value-added resellers (VARs). This combo relies on Notes to overcome ACT!'s data transportation shortcomings.

MOST GCM'S TALK TO EACH OTHER, BUT NOT MUCH ELSE.

In addition to their data swapping capabilities, most GCMs offer greater database capacity and more customization options than their ICM cousins. In fact, several GCM products are complex enough to be sold by VARs who customize and install the very same software that's available on retail shelves.

Do GCMs meet sales automation requirements? Close (in a few cases), but no cigar.

In my experience, a few GCMs will suffice for very basic sales automation needs; for instance, if all you are automating is a small sales force with a relatively unsophisticated sell. Try to integrate customer service functions into your automation system and you pretty much eliminate the GCM category from consideration. Want to carefully measure sales process steps to identify why sales reps of apparently similar capabilities are performing at such different levels? You're pretty much out of luck, here, too. Need a fully relational database with a powerful report-writing program to really slice and dice customer and market information? Still out of luck. Want a very open database structure built for easy import and export of data to and from different software programs? Most GMCs move data only through predesigned paths.

GCMs come packaged in more than a box. Most come with hidden constraints that flex a lot less than cardboard. In my travels among sales automation clients who've been down the road at least once before, I hear little but disappointment among GCM users, most of it regarding unmet expectations.

"I thought I'd be able to run this report this way."

"I can't get the data I want out of the system.

"It's fine if you want everything the way it's set up, but I can't change it to fit our business.

"Boy, did we get sold a bill of goods."

"Boy, did we get sold a bill of goods."

Unfortunately, "we got sold a bill of goods" and similar comments come up far too often. A primary reason, perhaps *the* primary reason for so much overselling, is that sales automation requires non-technical types to evaluate and buy technology. And even IT, when involved in the selection process, typically lacks the tools to evaluate sales automation technology on its merits; instead, they use evaluation criteria intended for other types of software that perform far simpler tasks. Of course, many IT departments view sales automation as a simple task. Salespeople themselves are simple, right? And who wants to waste time on sales when we haven't exhausted all the possible ways accounting can count our money?

The overselling issue comes up so frequently among GCM purchasers for three reasons:

1. *Most GCM software meets **some** sales automation requirements*—enough for *some* software developers in this

category and *some* VARs to take out the truth stretcher and represent their products as sales automation-certified.

2. *GCMs are products, not solutions.* If it's easy enough for you to use it out of the box, it's too simple to provide effective sales automation support.

3. *Most VARs selling GCMs are pretty low-octane outfits.* Not to denigrate those few VARs that do understand how to design, engineer and implement sales automation, but the great majority don't see very far beyond software. A good way to spot a good VAR, whether for GCMs or real sales automation solutions, is to look for an outfit that is also a Microsoft Solutions Partner, which usually speaks well of its ability to engineer and implement more than shrink-wrapped, Software R Us packages.

The VAR problem is particularly vexing. When I first entered the sales automation business, I was trying to limit my efforts to conceptual and functional design, believing I could hand off the technical implementation to VARs for the software products specified. Makes sense, doesn't it? Let people who sell and service the product and work with it every day configure it. I still get migraines thinking about that gaffe.

"Hey, can't make money sitting around the office designing implementation details." Not even for a stiff hourly fee. "Gotta sell, sell, sell!"

"Whadda ya mean, build a link to this other program. We do sales automation, not IT."

"Send our best tech person to the next meeting? You already got our best tech."

The principal thrust of GCM resellers appears to be sell, sell, sell! Market, market, market! And push product, not solutions.

Turns out my bad experiences aren't unique, either. I later became friends with the distribution channel manager for one of the better sales automation software developers. He complains to me constantly that he can't find resellers ready and willing to provide solutions, as opposed to just selling product at the highest possible markup.

Unfortunately, sales automation is a business where we can, if we try hard enough, believe we're buying a product. That's especially true when we're under the influence of companies anxious to sell us products. To me, and to many of the users I've encountered, GCMs are products, not solutions. Buy them, and you'll probably wind up an unhappy camper, with lots of unhappy people around you.

And to software resellers who rush customers into buying software, not solutions, here's a thought. In a couple of years, this industry will start to mature. The "pigeons" you target will be gone. Most first-time systems will be sold. Those who did it wrong the first time will be out to do it right. And how are you going to approach these customers a second time?

There's a reason Sherman didn't march through Georgia a second time.

Too bad the technically skilled and responsible VARs (and there are some out there) have to wade through the cow pies left by their less principled, less skilled peers.

Although GCMs are rarely good candidates for sales automation software support, you may have to defend *not* using these systems to the people around you (and over you) who are uninitiated in the whys and wherefores of sales automation. Plus, GCMs are adequate for some small businesses with a lim-ited number of users and no plans to advance to enterprise sales automation. So we should talk about the key players in this category, despite category limitations.

Here's what I see out there.

The off-the-shelf version of GoldMine may look great at first glance—until you discover that it too lacks a fully relational database, limiting its capabilities to manage more than relatively simple data structures. The shrink-wrapped version also limits users to a single-screen format per database, making effective use for both sales and customer service virtually impossible. And it lacks basic computational capabilities in all but select data fields, preventing you from imbedding calculations into your database for analysis and report-writing purposes.

(As I complete final edits on this puppy, GoldMine is introducing a new version 4.0 of the software. The new stuff can run on client-server networks, and the company claims it will synchronize with a variety of minicomputer and mainframe corporate databases. But remote users are still stuck with a less-than-relational database. Old paradigm stuff. Keep headwork at headquarters, cuz the field people ain't up to it. For me, that still leaves GoldMine among the ranks of GCMs, rather than up with the big boys and girls in the next software category.)

Maximizer does have a relational database, but lacks the requisite process management capabilities. The program also lacks a serious report-writing function.

TeleMagic offers relatively little flexibility in report-writing and analysis, and doesn't meet my expectations for either telemarketing or non telemarketing applications. It does, however, tie into several major accounting packages, which in certain applications gives it an advantage over others in this category. But it's old technology and getting older by the month.

And ACT! with Lotus Notes is proof that two wrongs don't make a right. From a customer data management standpoint, ACT! isn't competitive, even in the inadequate-for-sales-automation

GCM category. And Lotus Notes? I don't believe Notes has any positive role to play in sales automation. Notes is groupware—software that facilitates internal communication. It may do a helluva job there, but not in sales automation, primarily because Notes lacks a relational database capable of transporting linked tables of relational sales automation data. Even the several developers of higher end (than ACT!) sales automation programs that combine with Notes have to do a lot of fancy footwork to overcome problems created by moving relational data over a nonrelational database.

PEDDLING DATABASE MARKETING AND E-MAIL SOFTWARE FOR SALES AUTOMATION PURPOSES CONFUSES SOME CUSTOMERS.

Unfortunately, the sales automation industry has done a poor job combining customer data management with corporate e-mail. That's left a gaping opening for sellers of Notes and sales automation packages to march in with "the solution." And to some corporate types, many of whom still care more about e-mail than sales automation, the pitch sounds good. But to my ears, this pitch sounds like the late Tiny Tim. Thin and odd.

Bottom line—the only reason any groupware (aside from Microsoft Exchange) should ever enter into a sales automation consideration is because it is already installed. But until groupware developers such as IBM and Novel® (Groupwise) start using open architecture, relational database—don't try to meld them. You'll sacrifice too many sales automation benefits. And if any sales representative tries to sell you a "sales automation" system based on anyone's groupware (again, except for Microsoft Exchange), grab your wallet and take an aerobically correct walk in the opposite direction. Or tell them to take a hike.

Why the exemption for Microsoft Exchange? Because Exchange can transport relational databases. Microsoft is the only groupware developer that seems to understand groupware programs are not islands unto themselves.

Relationship Managers (RMs)

Moving up the sales automation software ladder a bunch more rungs, we reach relationship management software. Here we finally encounter programs capable of providing robust support for sales automation, even enterprise sales automation.

So why didn't we start with RMs and skip all the other stuff? *Because RMs represent only a tiny fraction of the sales automation software being purchased today.*

RM sales are lagging for several reasons:

- *Cost.* RMs typically cost $1,000 per station or more, and that represents a significant reduction over the past two years. GCMs, in contrast, go in the low hundreds.

- *Complexity.* Most RMs require a client-server network environment (which I'll discuss in just a bit, so please don't suffer techno-anxiety). In fact, being able to run with a client-server database may be the single most distinguishing feature of RMs. Client-server database products far outperform their PC cousins such as Access, Paradox and Clipper.

- *User awareness and understanding.* RMs are the new kids on the block in software that purports to support sales automation. Plus, the industry information pipeline to software buyers is still under construction.

- *Effort to implement.* You can't use RM programs out of the box. They require customization, which requires advance planning and a serious investment of the user organization's time. Hard commodities to come by in today's go-go, lean staffing, corporate environments.

- *Commitment to doing it right.* Most of all, RMs have such a small slice of the software pie because they represent a *commitment* to sales automation and an *acknowledgment* that sales automation is so much more than running down to Software R Us, buying a gross or two of a "safe choice," and dumping it down to the field like farmers droping feed into a trough.

While all of these factors contributing to RMs' weak market penetration are distressing, the widespread lack of commitment to doing things right may be most distressing. At least I find it so. Despite sales automation's well-documented bad track record, organizations are still lining up to repeat their predecessors' bad experiences with doing sales automation "on the cheap." Cheap in terms of money. Cheap in terms of time. Being a born-again Midwesterner, this reminds me of the true story about the long line of turkeys that wanted to get out of the rain. The lead bird decided to walk up the chute of a corn auger to the "safety" of a grinder, which reduced it to cattle feed. The flock followed in parade order…Hey, at least they stayed dry.

So it is with sales automation. One organization after another walks up the chute, voluntarily. No one's holding a gun to their head. Sad, to say the least.

So what do RMs provide that lesser categories don't to increase the chance of sales automation success? The following checklist describes the attributes of RM software. Use it to see where your sales automation system—or one you're thinking about buying—ranks on the "RM scale." Too many missing checks mean you might need to switch software or renew your software search.

RALATIONSHIP MANAGEMENT SOFTWARE ATTRIBUTES

Relational databases, without which effective data management is frustrating at best, impossible at worst.

Built for networking, in most cases a client-server environment.

Sophisticated remote synchronization that allows accurate, reliable and selective integration of user data.

Power to run large, complex databases that manage such data as customer use of competitive products, capital equipment inventories with projected replacement dates, full product lists with prices and configuration options, and detailed purchase histories.

Flexibility that permits significant customization of databases to meet user criteria—and customization of screens so sales and customer service don't have to operate from the same view (they can't).

Scalability that allows use of different versions of the same software program on laptops and client-server networks.

Adaptability to different database languages, facilitating communication with corporate legacy systems and integration with other application systems.

Opportunity management facilities that determine the timing and nature of future actions based on the outcomes of preceding sales, service and marketing process steps.

Pipeline management that lets sales, marketing and management accurately project future revenues and react to anticipated variations up or down.

Process management that can measure step-by-step outcomes, not just sales results—a tremendous benefit for training and personnel evaluation as well as sales and marketing.

Statistical analysis capabilities for capturing the meaning behind data; beyond a "data container."

Not every RM system delivers all these features. But the good ones deliver most or all of them. No question that RM systems cost much more than "shrink-wrapped" solutions, but when you consider their cost relative to the total cost of supporting a field sales person or a service representative for a year, they're worth it (okay, some are so expensive that even I can't cost-justify them). And when you consider their cost relative to the money wasted on marketing the wrong products the wrong way to the wrong customers—a frequent result of working without sufficient customer input—most RMs are a downright bargain. And they're still coming down in price.

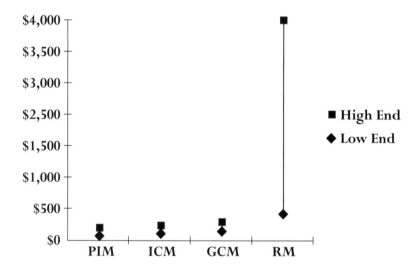

Price ranges by category.

Top entries in the category include Clarify's family of relationship management products, Onyx, Aurum Customer Relationship, TeamWorks from Optima Technologies, Pivotal's Pivotal Relationship, Saratoga Systems' Avenue and Siebel

Systems' Sales Enterprise. A well-financed startup company, SalesLogix®, has introduced a middle-weight (for this category), value-priced product of the same name. If you read trade magazines, you may have seen the ads. They feature the president of SalesLogix and pound home the point that this is the same guy who brought us ACT! (before he sold his company to Symantec). Perhaps not a wise strategy with the many users shedding ACT! for beefier software. Another new "middle-weight" RM entry to try is Sales Continuum 98 from IPC/Pipestream, Technologies®.

And while I'm trying to focus on best of breed, I have to mention one "near miss": Client Vision from WinSales®. If it ever gets redirected and refined, it would join SalesLogix in presenting a value-priced alternative to typically more expensive RM programs.

Client Vision offers a remarkably flexible database structure that users can reshape, virtually at will. It's like Silly Putty with a backbone. It also has the industry's best process management potential—if mortals could figure out how to program it, that is, and therein lies the problem. It's a brilliant program in search of a user interface. Oh yeah, and horrible documentation. An engineering marvel with rough edges all over the place.

WinSales apparently ran out of capital before it could complete and refine the program. The good news is that Magic Solutions®, a larger and better financed developer of help desk software, recently purchased WinSales. That will hopefully lead to a sandpaper (sand-blasting?) job to smooth off all the rough edges and make it explicable to those of us lacking "double-e" degrees. That, plus some marketing dollars behind it, might propel Client Vision right up the flagpole in the RM category.

Customer Service Systems

Customer service automation systems encompass two different software categories: help desk software and field service software. Both differ significantly in features and database structure from sales automation software. Both are also significantly more complex than most sales automation software. But the realization that sales and service need to share information seamlessly, on a real-time basis, is taking root on all three sides of the fence.

Software developers are playing catch-up with combining sales and service functions. But combined sales/service platforms are already available from several high-end RM system developers, including Aurum and Siebel Systems, and initial offerings affordable to organizations with less than four digits' worth of sales/service automation users are starting to appear. Perhaps the most promising is from Clientele, an Oregon company recently purchased by Platinum Software®. Clientele is adding sales automation to an excellent help desk program, with launch scheduled for right about the time this book arrives in bookstores all over the world (too bad sarcasm doesn't translate well). Another promising entry-to-come is the newly announced joint venture between SalesLogix and Opis®, developer of another fine help desk program.

Beyond these two options, a new, combined sales/service product from WinSales/Magic Solutions might help jump-start this new category. But look for it to be more expensive than either the Clientele combo or SalesLogix/Opis.

Related Systems Issues

Considerable confusion remains regarding the role of other types of data management software in sales automation. Much of the confusion is created by marketers of other types of software who don't appreciate sales automation systems cutting into their sales, or who don't understand sales automation at all. While I don't want to write a book about software, we need to spend enough time to clear up this confusion and discriminate between genuinely complementary software and the "smoke" bellowed forth by potential losers in the marketing-related software business.

To clear up the confusion about related software and systems, we have to risk more confusion by engaging in "tech talk" that I'd rather avoid. But, we gotta do what we gotta do. So put your seat belt back on and pay close attention to the road we're taking. I'll try to keep it light. (If you're an IT professional, please skip this section entirely. You won't learn a thing by reading it, and you'll save yourself a severe case of heartburn from reading incomplete, oversimplified descriptions of stuff that's near and dear to your heart. I just want sales, service and marketing folks to have a concept of what you're thinking and talking about in your language while they're thinking and talking in their languages about sales automation.)

Here we go. You're a one-person office. You have one computer. That computer has what's called an *operating system*, or OS. (And now you know how they came up with "DOS"—it stands for "da operating system.") Your operating system is probably Windows 95. Or maybe Windows 3.1. If it's Mac, you've been drawing pictures instead of reading, so you can nod out again. This operating system provides core commands like "turn on" and "turn off," "print this" and "fetch that file from the hard drive." It also provides the basic user interface—what users see and whether they enter keyboard commands, use a mouse, or both. That's why Windows looks so different from DOS on your screen.

Now, you can't do much with just Windows alone. You need application programs that perform some task or other, probably a whole bunch of related tasks. You buy these programs at Software R Us. Or from a mail-order catalogue. Or from your business computer resource. Unless they came preloaded on your computer. But most of those preloaded programs aren't very businesslike, except for Microsoft Office.

Nice and cozy. You. Your operating system. Your application programs. An island unto yourself. Until you plug a phone line into the modem that came with your computer and sign up for Internet service. Suddenly, you're a cyber-citizen.

Oh, I almost forgot. You bought yourself a popular PIM to keep your calendar straight and clear your desk of that telephone number holding device. Neat program. It has it's own database, everything it needs, self-contained, except for a word processor. But no matter, because it links right up to your existing word processor.

You grow. A second person comes to work in your office. Or maybe you had to go out and get an office so a second person could work with you. Now you have two computers. But only one can be hooked up to the printer at any one time. And exchanging files by trading diskettes gets old fast, especially when you create this humongo file that won't split, but that's too big for a diskette. So you buy two network cards,

IF YOU'RE A GROWTH COMPANY, BUY A SALES AUTOMATION SYSTEM THAT'S BIGGER THAN YOU ARE.

one for each computer, and a network cable to run between your computers. You spend five minutes installing the cards and a day-and-a-half loading this dumb software program that came with the cards, plus another half-day and three tech support calls configuring Windows 95 for network use. Now you have a *peer network*. You can both use the same printer. You can rifle through each other's files. You can even send each other e-mail without using telephone lines or the Internet. Best of all, you get to keep using all of your same applications software.

Oh, and your partner also had a PIM. You tried to network yours first. Dump city. Tried your partner's. No dice. Ran down to Software R Us and bought two copies of a popular ICM that says it networks. Dicey, but it will do. Convenient like your PIM. Ready to run right out of the box, its own database and all.

Your business blossoms. You add more employees. Each one gets a computer with a network card and a network cable running to these network hubs you had to buy to plug everybody into one network. But then things start getting weird. No one knows which file is on what computer. People take to shouting, "Who moved the blankety-blank file for XYZ company off my hard drive?" and the like. So you grab the Yellow Pages, look under "Computer Consultants," and call the one with the least obnoxious ad.

The consultant arrives, strokes his beard, and says, "You need a real network. A LAN." And you say, "Say, I just happen to be reading this great book that talks about LANs and "LAN-sync," and here's this picture, and…" The consultant pats you on the head and says, "You'll be okay in the morning. I'll handle this for you." A few weeks and many thousands of dollars later, you have a real server that holds everyone's files in a common directory. You can get into everyone else's files. But they can't get into yours, thanks to this neat security system. You still get to keep your Windows operating system and application programs. But you now have this cranky software program that "administers" the network. Pain in the butt.

But on the brighter side, you went back to Software R Us and said, "We want the best contact manager on the shelf." You got it. Bought one for every person dealing with customers, sales and service both. Runs great on the network, too. Uses something called a "shared directory." Everyone uses their own software but shares the same database. Reps on the road can even tie in their laptops to update data. But the service people are griping. They say they can't use it 'cause it's set up wrong for service calls. Can't do much analysis on it, either. "I thought that dumb clerk said this was the best. Friend of mine keeps showing me how they can pinpoint what's going wrong and what's going right in their sales process. Why can't we?"

Growth, growth, growth. Before long, your network has slowed to a crawl. It takes five minutes to download the fax template to order lunch. That contact manager you bought can't hold all the customer data you're generating, either. Gotta do something different. This time you call the biggest ad in the Yellow Pages. Slick consultant. Nice clothes. Tells you it's time for a real network, as in client-server. You gasp at the price. And you gasp even louder when you hear that you'll have to add yet another operating system called "NT Server." When you hear the price, all of a sudden you love Windows 95. You shudder and ask if "NT" stands for "no trouble." Consultant chuckles. You don't.

But you do it. New network server (that's a computer) loaded with NT Server. Then there's this razzle-dazzle new question-writing language that queries your new system called SQL (short for Sequel). Plus a built-in database called "Sequel Server." "Wait a minute," you complain, "we're up to two servers, two Sequels, and I'm confused as hell."

"Relax," your consultant says, "don't sweat the details."

"But," your consultant adds, "that store-bought contact management program won't run on NT Server. Won't operate on an Sequel Server database, either. Friend of mine's a sales automation consultant." You sense it coming and grab your wallet.

Sure enough, the sales automation software programs that the sales automation consultant shows you cost more *per station* than you invested to start the business (if you don't count all the credit card bills you rang up). And there's this sales automation "server" station that's going to cost close to ten grand for just the software license (more than you invested including the credit cards). But hey, you've got the dough now. Besides, the automation consultant assures you that you made an excellent decision going with Microsoft's NT Server and Sequel database instead of migrating to a UNIX® operating system and using a UNIX core database written in IT-friendly languages such as Oracle, Sybase or Informix. If you'd chosen any of the alternatives, you'd have very little sales automation software to choose from, and you'd have to pay a very lot for what you could get.

Then the other shoe drops. Your friendly sales automation consultant informs you that you're not ready to pick a system yet because you don't know what you need. Something about "process flow" and "data maps." Bleary-eyed by now, you just roll over and say, "Find out what we need, BUT DO IT FAST." Two months later, you finally get the opportunity to spring for new sales automation software. It doesn't come in a box. Instead, it comes with a technician to configure and install it. That's another six weeks.

So, from your humble beginnings with a simple operating system and an out-of-the-box, self-contained PIM, you've now advanced to an expensive sales automation software system with multiple Sequels, multiple servers (one's actually the network server, but you're too confused by now to make that distinction) and enough twists to give a snake arthritis.

Is this progress?

Youuuu betcha.

Dog-ear these pages so you can reread them before your next meeting with IT. Hopefully you'll be better able to understand what they're babbling about, and they'll be better able to understand what you're babbling about. For every time you've said, "They just don't understand customers," IT has said, "They just don't understand technology."

Sales-automation-speak has to include more than a little IT-speak. Hope you grasped several of the key words. Besides, all you have to do is mix in an occasional word of theirs while you're speaking your language. That works.

What doesn't work is the new head of IT you hired after you bought all this fancy new hardware. His first words were,

"This will never do. You have to decide on a new accounting system first. Then we'll have to look at redoing all this 'customer management' stuff to fit the accounting package."

Your first words back are, "You're fired." You thought you didn't know much about information systems. The IT "expert" hasn't grasped, yet, what you have intuitively understood about your business and about business in general. *Customers come first.* And that doesn't apply just to marketing and sales. It's the guiding principle around which everything in your business revolves—even information systems and accounting.

Data Warehouses

"Data dumps," as some of us disparagingly refer to customer data warehouses, have but a limited role in sales automation. There's nothing inherently wrong with data warehouses—if you have enough *usable* customer data to require such a vast repository and if all of your customer knowledge can be reduced to quantitative data (in which case you may have another serious problem).

Most customer data warehouses wind up holding large volumes of unusable or old and unreliable data. They really do become data dumps, with mounds of useless data piled over mounds of data piled over higher mounds of data that we've forgotten we ever had and don't remember why we collected. And customarily missing in the "slag heap" that accumulates in these data coffers is textual, graphical and other non-numerical data that's often the backbone of customer knowledge.

Data warehouses hold "history" files. They don't manage opportunities. They don't account for the "whys" of customer behavior that tell us what to do next. Instead, they hold the "whats" that tell us what happened in the past. Lest you think I scoff at quantitative, historical data, let me hasten to add that I do believe that "old numbers" are very valuable—for the purposes of research and analysis. But they are inappropriate for the real-time data management requirements of sales automation. Let me repeat myself. DON'T USE A DATA WAREHOUSE TO MANAGE REAL-TIME DATA!

Outside of warehousing historical data, I predict that data warehousing will turn out to be a very transitory trend, quickly becoming obsolete once we master the art of moving data across disparate operating systems and software platforms—and once we reorient ourselves to using "why" knowledge that explains the "what" data," instead of just guessing at whatever's behind the "what" data. I admit, they'll still have a role, but we'll stop abusing data warehouses by forcing them to do what they weren't designed to do—namely, manage real-time data.

Marketing databases

"Marketing database" is such a wonderful euphemism. It's like those words with the silent first letter, "knot" or "psyche" or whatever. But with "marketing database" it's the whole first word that's dropped: there's a silent "direct" in front of "marketing database." (Direct) marketing databases aren't really designed for marketing use, but for direct mail and telemarketing use and for analysis that helps us do more and better direct mail and telemarketing. Not to get fussy over terms, but last time I looked, direct mail was a communication tactic for popping the rivets on people's mailboxes and telemarketing was a sales tactic that we all loved to hate.

But, you might ask, don't (direct) marketing databases have valuable data to contribute to sales automation? Not much. Your average (direct) marketing database relies heavily on third-party data such as compiled mailing lists, subscription lists, trade show lists, department of motor vehicles information, census data, extrapolations from census data, extrapolations from extrapolations from census data....

While (direct) marketing databases and direct marketing itself can supplement certain sales automation efforts, they're more what sales automation is replacing. The pity is that many organizations build (direct) marketing databases instead of sales automation systems, assuming they'll get the same benefits. To the contrary, effective sales automation subordinates mass, addressable communication to much more individualized customer marketing strategies made possible by the presence of direct-from-customer data.

(DIRECT) MARKETING DATABASES HAVE A VERY MUNDANE PURPOSE.

I do respect direct marketing's accomplishments. If I didn't, I'd have to renounce years of my own work, including some I haven't done yet. But I'm focusing on sales automation because I want to get closer to customers than direct marketing allows, and because I have a very keen sense of the boundary between "direct" and the true customer marketing that sales automation enables.

Management Decision Systems

The term "management decision systems (MDS)" is also quite a euphemism. This time, though, instead of a word missing, there's an incorrect word present. A management *decision* system is really a management *data* system. And we're talking quantitative data, almost exclusively.

A true management decision system should be a highly refined extract of customer knowledge and financial and operating data. Unfortunately, most MDS are long on financial and operating data; void of any customer knowledge, aside from raw, quantitative data with no "whys" behind the data; and used to make statistically based decisions based on uninformed guesses about the reasons for the numbers. In other words, *most MDS treat symptoms rather than causes.*

Purveyors of (direct) marketing database software and services are heavily promoting MDS as an extension of their core product. But remember, (direct) marketing databases contain information *about* customers, not information *from* customers. Before your CEO buys into the idea that building an MDS is an appropriate response to your need to get ever closer to customers, ask him or her how many errant pieces of direct mail they received yesterday. Then ask if they want to base their management decisions on the database that brought them their junk mail.

But maybe we should cut the (direct) marketing database industry some slack. They have to recoup their investment in all that expensive hardware and software somehow.

AN ANIMAL UNTO ITSELF

Introducing sales automation into our organizations challenges the beliefs, customs and work processes that are deeply ingrained in most corporate cultures. For example:

Sales automation development starts at the point of customer contact. Who would think of developing a corporate information system without basing it on whatever information corporate management wants out of it? Anyone serious about sales automation would. Sales automation development must start where customer information is gathered, then work back to corporate (or to the central information-gathering point). That's exactly opposite of how we're accustomed to working, especially in the IT environment. Attempting to maintain traditional information system design parameters by working from "corporate out" has led to many expensive sales automation failures. (In fact, I know of no organization that has engineered successful sales automation by starting at corporate and working out, although many have tried and many more continue to try this route.)

Sales automation reverses customer data flow. Sales automation reverses the primary direction of customer data flow. Traditionally, corporate staff send data to sales and service. Under sales automation, sales and service pass along data to corporate. Similarly, sales automation redistributes the volume of customer data held at various points in the organization. Traditionally, corporate staff held the most customer data, followed by field management, followed by relationship managers. Under sales automation, relationship managers hold the biggest share of customer information, with field managers and corporate staff holding progressively smaller amounts. Corporate management receives only low-volume extracts and data high points that will help them think strategically (rather than arithmetically, as many corporate managements think).

Despite all the new data gathered under sales automation, in some cases, an effective sales automation system may actually decrease the total volume of customer information moving from point-to-point. That's because it moves information more directly and only actionable data is moved on to each successive level. The bulk of the data that relationship managers capture aids only the sales and service processes and the one-to-one marketing initiatives that sales and service, rather than marketing, customarily implement. The smaller share of customer data that does go back to corporate—such as sales volume, "in the pipeline" sales projections, competitive intelligence, customer impressions of products and services, early warnings about shifts in buyer behavior, reasons why we're doing better with some customer groups than others, the impact of our advertising and promotion, new product and service opportunities—is extraordinarily valuable, but it's also very low in volume. That's especially true compared to transferring gobs of statistical data that few ever look at or use.

Sales automation inverts the traditional data pyramid. Beyond the specifics just detailed, most organizations conceptualize information management as a corporate function and selling and servicing as field functions. Accordingly, most corporate people hold a subconscious perception that concentrations of any type of organizational data, including customer data, are naturally a corporate-level function. Sales automation, carried beyond a simple sharing of contact information, directly challenges this presumption.

The charts on the following two pages show the change in information concentration that sales automation can bring about. These have elicited many a "gulp" from first-time viewers. Recently, I met with a client from one of the companies most responsible for the "desktop revolution." His organization was attempting to establish a customer data warehouse at HQ—and failing. We'd discussed the problems of doing so previously, including the possibility that data warehousing was the wrong solution, but I hadn't communicated my concerns in a meaningful way. So I showed him these charts. He put his head in his hands and said, "No wonder this isn't working."

Then, being the merciful type, I added, "You've reinvented IBM." Low blow, I admit.

CORPORATE-CENTRIC CUSTOMER DATA FLOW

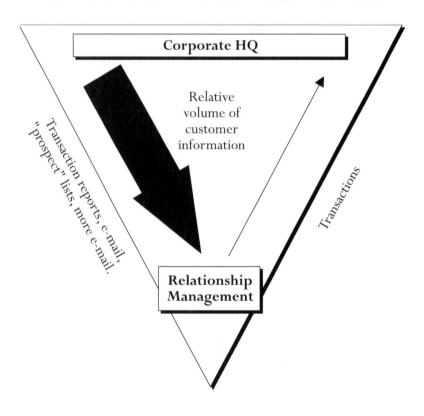

Customer-centric Data Flow

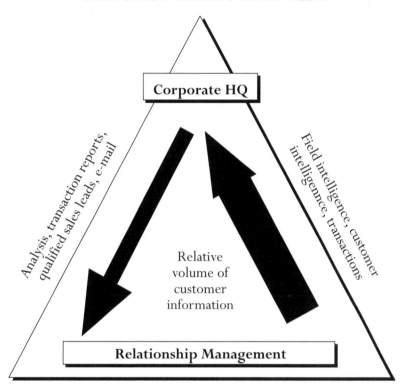

In a sales automation setting, relationship management needs come first. The principal users of sales automation are relationship managers, primarily in sales and service. They already have full-time jobs, other than acquiring and managing data. Yet corporate can't take data gathering off their hands, because who else would gather data at the point of customer contact? Some data can be acquired through telemarketing, but not the most and not the best stuff. Relationship managers have to mine for that, which means they need extra hours in their day. *Something has to give, and that something is the administrative demands placed on relationship managers.*

Sales automation *must* be designed to lighten the relationship managers' load—by making reporting faster and easier, by automating quote/proposal preparation and all manner of customer communication, by speeding up the process of obtaining product and service information, and by shortening the time required to communicate internally. Ask even your best sales reps what percentage of their time is spent on these tasks. Expect the worst and you still may be stunned by how much time they spend "off-line" and away from customers. Include reading corporate e-mail in the "time wasted" calculation and the numbers get outright scary.

The sticking point here is that *most organizations are unaccustomed to taking care of relationship management needs first and corporate management needs second.* Being unprepared for this switch in priorities usually leads to assessing sales automation needs in closed corporate meetings, with little or no contact-level input. In which case, the sales automation they come up with inevitably places additional off-line responsibilities on sales and service, rather than lightening their load.

Among the most thoroughly depressing meetings I've ever attended was a milestone sales automation project review meeting at the corporate offices of an international service marketer. Very telling was the fact that only IT people plus a token staff marketer were invited (I was uninvited, but attended as someone's guest). No sales representation in sight. No field marketing presence there. No surprise, after four years and over $10 million invested, that all they'd accomplished was a hodgepodge "home brew" management decision system with barely a shred of field sales usability. And when someone naively asked, "Will this system would work for the field?" the snappy reply was, "As long as they can print their direct mail letters, they'll be happy."

Two fries short of a Happy Meal.

They all need a reality check. So does their organization, which stands to spend millions more for the privilege of falling further behind the competition—and losing a good piece of their sales force when they belatedly introduce this mess that should never have seen the light of day.

For organizations unaccustomed and unprepared to consider relationship management needs first, sales automation and attendant customer-driven marketing strategies will inevitably clash with the corporate culture. Attempts to "bend the rules" and implement sales automation as a corporate system with relationship management tentacles usually follow. *Better that such organizations not attempt to implement sales automation until they're ready and able to change their internal priorities.* And if they do, they'd better bring along a giant dustpan and big brooms to clean up all the messes.

Sales automation is not a flexible and forgiving environment when its focus drifts far from relationship management needs to management information wants, or when it's turned into a big stick for keeping sales in line. Done right, it's an enormously powerful tool. Used as a backdrop for filling corporate information larders or beating up on sales, sales automation actually can do lots of damage to the organization. And a good measure of that damage is only reversible over time—the time it takes to win back the trust of your sales and service people, which won't be anytime soon.

THE BIG OPPORTUNITY

HOW BIG IS BIG?

Big. Damn big. Not golf ball or tennis ball or baseball or softball or basketball big. But medicine ball big. As long as someone takes the time and trouble to inflate the thing, that is. Listen to the case of a $7 billion electronics manufacturer cited in the Harvard Business Review:

> "The electronics concern installed a sales support system for more than 500 salespeople. Sales rose 33%, sales force productivity rose 31%, and sales force attrition dropped 40%. The reduced attrition alone produced savings in recruiting and training costs that paid for the company's $2.5 million investment in less than 12 months."[7]

---

[7] Rowland T. Moriarty and Gordon S. Swartz, "Automation to Boost Sales and Marketing." *Harvard Business Review* (January-February 1989).

This article appeared in early 1989, when sales automation technology was in its infancy. Not only would this system be better today, it would cost substantially less, perhaps only a half or a third of what it cost then.

More recently, Training magazine chronicled these sales automation successes:[8]

- Northern Telecom estimates a 15% increase in sales productivity due to sales automation.

- Polaroid reports that the "15 calls" it took sales to reach the right marketing person to answer a product question have virtually evaporated, now that field reps have laptops and e-mail. (Notice that this example cites sales reaching corporate, not vice versa.)

- Federal Express believes it saves upwards of a million dollars annually just on the cost of brochures now that it can custom-print tailored pieces for individual customers, rather than mass-printing and warehousing generic pieces.

But think back to the Introduction of this book and the high failure rate of sales automation projects (the Training article pegs the number at 70%). Obviously, lots of medicine balls are sitting out there deflated. Some just need inflating. Others have holes in them that need patching. Some are beyond patching. But even if you have to start over again from scratch, sales automation is worth it.

Why does sales automation have such astonishing potential? So much potential that so many organizations continue to try it, despite the bad track record? I could go on and on about all the wonderful outcomes sales automation can produce. Write a whole book about it. But I won't. I won't because there's

---

[8] Margaret Kaeter, "Building a Cyber Sales Force," *Training* (April 1996), pp. 37-42.

already too much "sales automation dreaming" going on out there, and we need to knock the stars out of our eyes and do more than talk the talk.

That said, some of this stuff is too good *not* to talk about. So I will. For a while. Then it's back into the challenges and the messy stuff.

Sales automation offers users astounding potential for four primary reasons:

Sales and marketing are still waiting for the industrial revolution. Actually, we're still in the stone age, but we're right at the mouth of the cave. From a process management standpoint, we have nowhere to go but up, and we have a *staggering* amount of room for improvement. After decades of management neglect, the revenue-producing side of business is about to get a heap of attention. In fact, a heap more than many of us are prepared to handle, because with that attention will come vastly increased *accountability* and *measurability*.

> IN PROCESS TERMS, SALES AND MARKETING MAY BE IN THE STONE AGE, BUT THEY'RE RIGHT AT THE MOUTH OF THE CAVE.

Before long, sales and marketing will be evaluating and re-evaluating their processes just like manufacturing and financial people do today. The goal? To keep working smarter and smarter to produce better and better outcomes with less and less investment and expense. And that's a job that's tailor-made for sales automation with its process management potential.

Sales automation can be your competitive edge. While more and more organizations are attempting to jump on the sales automation bandwagon, far more than half of them land on their you-know-what. And if you figure that 60% to 70% or more of the organizations in many businesses segments haven't yet taken their first leap, that leaves a small minority that have successfully implemented sales automation in a distinctly superior competitive position. The early bird does get the worm—and the worms are there for the pickin'.

The world, at least today's world, belongs to the efficient producers, and the early birds.

True, the sales automation movement is growing by leaps and bounds. But the number of *successful* implementations is growing at a much slower pace. That still leaves plenty of opportunity for companies in most industries to use sales automation as a pogo stick for leaping over the competition. Anytime you have a wide disparity among competing organizations in adoption of a critical new process, you're going to see winners and losers. The wider the disparity, the wider the gap between winners and losers. Just ask American car makers who failed to adopt modern process management techniques in the 1980s about that.

Sales automation affects both sides of the ledger. And the benefits on either the income or expense side are sufficient to quickly pay off investment in a well-designed sales automation system. Add up increased sales, decreased sales hiring and training costs, higher marketing ROI, reduced marketing and marketing communication expenditures, more productive time from staff in many functions, reduced communication expense, plus lots more, and the payoff can be big...really big.

Enterprise sales automation improves nearly every part of the organization. It's easy to babble on about "enterprise this" and "enterprise that," and I'm as guilty of this as the next person, maybe more so. So instead of waxing poetic about the wonders of sales automation, let me tell a still-unfolding story that beautifully illustrates sales automation's long arms.

The client of a process management consultant friend of mine was searching for a sales automation program. Marketing had evaluated perhaps a hundred or so, at least superficially, because they weren't finding anything that felt right for them. Management was getting edgy about the delay in finding a solution, while a significant percentage of the field sales reps were buying a popular shrink-wrapped ICM that wasn't a long-term solution (but often gets in the way of implementing a true solution). At my friend's recommendation, I was asked to help focus the client's search and recommend an appropriate sales automation system.

The first step was mapping the company's current customer data flow and learning its sales, service and marketing processes. Almost immediately, hints about the issues and opportunities began cropping up:

- Although it was technically capital equipment, customers considered the company's product a commodity that purchasing should buy.

- Sales reps, who traveled constantly, helped spec jobs and prepared bids and proposals. They didn't usually close deals, except for national contracts.

- The primary rep functions were to maintain good relationships, provide customers a liaison to service and manufacturing, and keep the company's hat in the ring at every sales and bid opportunity.

- Internal communication between customer service and sales was informal and haphazard.

- With no timely warning of serious service issues, sales frequently got "chopped off at the knees" when they arrived to see customers.

- Customer service was attached to the accounting system on dumb terminals.

- Customer service was also sending incorrect parts in approximately 15% of shipments, a major irritant to customers.

- The parts were incorrect because purchasing was buying components on a least-cost basis from a variety of suppliers, which made it necessary for manufacturing to switch components in midrun. Manufacturing was not keeping "string records" that identified the serial numbers of finished whole goods that contained like components.

- Manufacturing and product marketing (which focused on product design) needed "issues input" from customers so they could make the small refinements and larger scale product innovations needed to maintain their market leadership position.

Even if you've never monkeyed with sales automation before, you might well see the core issue bubbling up to the surface. This "sales automation" system needed to be centered on customer service, not sales. Service was the natural information hub.

Also, purchasing and manufacturing needed to get together and change the method of supplying components to the manufacturing line. The money saved in purchasing was less than the freight costs they "ate" as a result of shipping incorrect parts. And no way was shaving nickels and dimes from product cost worth aggravating so many customers.

Putting service, not sales, at the center of the system eliminated all but a tiny fraction of sales automation software from consideration. The open architecture necessary to pass data between service accounting and manufacturing eliminated even more. Identifying the software selected comes too close to potentially revealing the client, but I can guarantee you that it wasn't off-the-shelf software.

How far will this sales automation system reach, when fully implemented?

Into *customer service,* where it will be the core system for telephone support, parts shipment, customer issues management and internal communication with sales.

Into *sales,* where it will be the "contact manager" here and abroad, the keeper of complex price matrices for preparing bids and quotes, and the issues management pipeline.

> **IT'S RISKY TO ASSUME THAT SALES, NOT SERVICE, IS THE HUB OF A SALES AUTOMATION SYSTEM.**

Into *accounting,* where it will feed parts and shipping costs for billing and potentially extract information for customer service.

Into *manufacturing,* where it will draw information about which components are in which whole goods.

Into *product marketing* where it will deliver information on customer issues that can be converted into product revisions and new products.

And it could reach even further, if this organization wants to become even more customer-centered. As a result of sales automation, a good portion of the company will be better, faster, smarter, more accurate and more knowledgeable in dealings with customers. That's a far cry from lower-case ambitions such as getting 10% more calls from sales, knowing who's loafing out there or hooking 'em up to e-mail to give them instructions they can't ignore (wanna bet?)—some of the specious reasons used for getting into sales automation by organizations destined to become casualty statistics. Hey, at least their low level of effort is consistent with their low expectations.

SALES OPPORTUNITIES

Process management and process improvement—that's what sales automation contributes most to successfully acquiring, developing and retaining customers. Some might object to this characterization of sales in particular as a process. "Hey, selling is a gift. Right?" As we say in Minnesota, "Ya, sure."

Recently, I sat in a meeting and listened to a VAR for one of the higher-end, retail software packages insist that "sales is not a process; it's individual to everyone and you can't reduce it to process steps." The client winked at me as we left the room. Unbelievable. But that's how ingrained the view of "sales as a personality aberration" really is. Even some in the business of supporting the sales *process* claim they're doing otherwise. What, I don't know.

A training manager at one of this country's more successful vehicle manufacturers provided what I consider the last word about process in sales. My principal client contact and I were presenting the rough concept of a new sales automation system to this training manager and others. We were concerned because this individual should have been involved from day one, but he had been recently hired and this was the first opportunity we'd had to meet with him. We carefully explained how we'd focused the system on managing activities rather than customer facts, because sales process improvement was the principal opportunity.

When we finished, he leaned back, thought for a second, turned to my client and said to her,

> "Salespeople sell by process or by accident. Accidents don't happen often enough."

Amen.

Another recent event reminded me of how frequently we confuse "process" and "inborn selling skills." I was beginning a sales automation project for a telephone sales firm. One of the first steps was to listen to the reps, to capture the sequence and rhythm of their calls. One of the first calls I heard was made by a gentleman called "Ace" by his colleagues. You can guess why.

He placed a call to a good customer to sell an item costing over $1,000. Not bad, for over the telephone. I listened in awe as he worked through a beautifully structured sales pitch, taking time to answer objections and to match the product's attributes to the customer's taste and preferences (and purchase history). The call seesawed back and forth, until Ace found his opening and went for a trial close. Not quite. A bit more reinforcement. Another close. Got it. A warm thank-you. Then, a very careful presentation to confirm the buying decision and prevent buyer's remorse, including a follow-up communication with product details and supporting information. Beautifully done. But if I had asked Ace about his selling process, guaranteed he would have said, "What process?"

MOST GOOD SALESPEOPLE ARE MADE, NOT BORN.

Although some your best salespeople may appear to have a "gift" for selling, underneath their gift is almost always a bedrock foundation of steps they take to complete the sale. They're just so smooth and effortless that you never see them climbing these steps. But lacking that marriage of personality and process, which part of the equation would you want them to have? If you've ever been a sales manager, you answered "process" without a moment's hesitation.

Personality without process translates into "looks good but sells squat." Process, on the other hand, without the magic personality, describes your bread-and-butter salespeople. They're the ones sales automation helps most.

Sales Process Management

Every product or service requires a different sequence of steps. But for illustration, let's look at a typical business-to-business, capital goods chain of sales events to see how sales automation can provide incremental improvement every step of the way.

Qualification of initial inquiries.

Picking the wheat from the chaff becomes much easier when each inquiry received becomes a sales automation database record. Telephone qualifiers can increase their speed and accuracy working from electronic records. Both inbound and outbound tele-qualifiers follow a preset branching script that gets them to core questions as quickly as possible. They enter information received directly into preset database fields, make consistent determinations of which inquiries are really qualified, then load qualified sales leads directly onto sales rep databases via remote synchronization. They can even reactivate temporarily nonqualified responses for requalification at appropriate time intervals. Outbound tele-qualifiers can also auto-dial from computer-generated lists, which can increase their productivity substantially.

Sales call selectivity

Ever wonder why relationship managers often call on some relatively low volume accounts rather than key accounts? Could be for lots of reasons, but they're much less prone to neglect important relationships when they rely on database information to suggest whom they should call on next week and next month. And sales volumes aren't always the driving factor in call selection. New product introductions and special price offers may require call schedules based on specific product usage and particular customer needs. Taking two minutes to build a sales automation database query to find the right customers or prospects to call on is a heck of a lot more accurate than leaning back in your chair and saying, "Let's see…"

Call frequency

Whom we call on and how often are affected by a rep's like or dislike of specific customers, the customer's "tolerance" of limited attention from the relationship manager, convenience factors...you name it. If we analyzed our calls at year-end to compare call frequency with call impact, we'd almost certainly discover frequent occurrences of both overcoverage and undercoverage. Sales automation will let us predetermine our call frequency based on the projected impact of the call, and then adjust call frequency with a few mouse clicks or key strokes when situations change. It's the old Pareto Principle at work: we spend 80% of our sales time on 20% of our business...isn't that how it goes?

Focus is to sales what location is to real estate. How many times have all of us who have "carried the bag" wasted hard-to-schedule sales calls focusing on the wrong products or the wrong needs or the wrong concerns? Too many times to remember. Funny how our mistake dawns on us minutes after the call, when we're finally able to put two and two together. Not that sales automation is going to add two and two and give relationship managers the score at the door, but a good database will prompt relationship managers to recall key issues and help establish the right call strategy. Two minutes reviewing a computerized customer record before the call can cut two years off the close—if there ever is a close.

Continuity

Sales automation builds customer relationships. No customer likes to hear from their sales rep phrases like, "Did we talk about...?" "Did I mention...?" "Did you ask me...?" or "Now I remember..." Continuity is about being buttoned-down, professional, respectful, competent. It's also about keeping the sales dialog on track from call to call, not wasting half the time remembering where we left off or what we discussed last time we met. The continuity provided by sales automation is particularly helpful in making the transition from one relationship manager to another, with a minimum loss of sales momentum and customer knowledge.

AMONG THE BEST WAYS TO INCREASE SALES PRODUCTIVITY IS TO UNCHAIN REPS FROM THEIR DESKS.

More customer time implies less time doing administrative chores—expense reports and call reports and status reports and rolling forecasts and whatever else management dreams up. More customer time even involves spending less time on some types of customer work, such as preparing customer quotes and proposals, product research, customer correspondence and responding to customer inquiries.

Sales automation automates all these functions and more. It can save a sales rep hours per week, perhaps a day per week.

Improved close ratios

We don't up our close ratios by learning "19 surefire closing techniques" or reading *I Made a Million Dropping My Pen on Ready-to-Sign Contracts*. Increased close ratios result from understanding which opportunities are most likely to close and for what reasons—and pursuing them (or not) accordingly. Many times, the die was cast in preceding calls or by the entire preceding sales process. We can read about it in our call records, if we keep them and keep them accessible.

Can sales automation predict successful closes? Not infallibly, but relationship managers who take the time to populate customer and prospect data records can read situations much more clearly than those who don't. These data-conscious relationship managers can then focus on their best opportunities and walk away from long shots. A simple sales automation spread sheet program tied to each customer's record can calculate future value based on the probability of getting the business, at what price and for what volume. Running that report will not only reshape call schedules, but also automate sales forecasting and increase forecasting accuracy.

Increased lifetime value

Think back to Ace. He exemplifies the impact of sales automation on customer lifetime value, without even using sales automation. He does what few sales reps can do: he remembers his customers, knows instinctively whom to target when with what, knows their "openings" and their defenses, structures his sales calls, sells in incremental steps, closes gracefully, reinforces his close and follows up after the sale. Only trouble is you can't go out and hire Ace. And thanks to the negative perception of sales internally, the quality of potential sales hires has diminished over the years. Who wants to be in sales? The job is hard enough, without all the guff you take.

The biggest difference between good and mediocre salespeople is often what they do after the initial sale. Sales automation helps salespeople less gifted than Ace perform more like him.

Improved customer retention

Reducing customer churn is top priority almost everywhere in business, but especially in sales. "Too many products to buy, too few new customers to buy them, too many competitors." Could become the marketing mantra for the new millennium. With the return on marketing dollars invested in customer acquisition shriveling up, while the return on investing in customer retention and development holds firm, *customer retention is evolving from a competitive strategy to a survival strategy.*

Lower sales force turnover

Rep churn is almost as expensive as customer churn, partly because the former leads to the latter. Good salespeople are hard to find, harder to hire and even harder to keep. What can we do about that? We can't increase the birthrate of star sales talent. We can't clone Ace. And even if we could, genetic re-engineering is even slower than corporate re-engineering. So we have to do the next best thing—increase productivity among the great "middle echelon" of moderately talented, less-than-superstar relationship managers.

Sales automation can *track and measure* individual sales process steps to identify "best practices" that midlevel relationship managers should emulate.

Sales automation can *identify process problems* for individual relationship managers, giving management the opportunity to provide highly targeted training support to address these weaknesses.

Sales automation-based process measurements can *predict the future success of new hires,* allowing management to end a terminal situation long before their intuition is confirmed by poor sales outcomes.

Sales automation *keeps relationship managers focused* (in part by keeping their managers focused). A relationship manager who can't get or stay focused is not long for his or her position.

Sales automation *provides a challenge* to relationship managers that can help keep their jobs fresh and help them maintain a sense of personal growth.

And one more thing. Sales automation *helps multiline or multidivisional users maintain "one face" to the customer.* Sort of like the left hand knowing what the right hand is doing. And one purchasing agent not getting successive calls from three representatives of the same company.

Okay, I did say "one more thing." But I can't leave this next stuff out. In manufacturing today, they use a process analysis approach called "theory of constraints," or TOC. What's TOC got to do with sales, marketing and sales automation? Everything.

TOC is all about finding and removing critical bottlenecks that impede the work flow. Almost every time I analyze a client's steps-to-the-sale—from marketing and public relations creating awareness of the seller to setting up new customers on back office accounting and logistics systems—I find bottlenecks. Constraints that restrict the throughput of customers. Big ones that are costing my clients far more than they're paying me; often far more than they're going to pay for sales automation in toto. Like when marketing spends millions to generate a gazillion sales leads, but sales can only qualify 25% of them to see if they're worth anything. The rest go to the round file. Like when it costs millions in sales expenses to close a gazillion new customers, but accounting can't clear their credit fast enough and logistics can't ship fast enough. So half-a-gazillion become ex-customers after one order.

Just recently, I sat down over lunch with a TOC consultant friend of mine, Bob Krausert. Manufacturing guy. Can triple production with no capital outlay for some clients. Problem is, as he was telling me, oftentimes clearing internal bottlenecks only creates new constraints in sales and marketing. Three times the production ain't worth much if you can't generate even a modest increase in sales. He wanted to compare work methods to see how we could work together. Darned if we aren't doing pretty much the same thing, Bob in the back office and me in the front office. I plan sales automation work flow the very same way he plans manufacturing work flow. Yeah, we can work together. He helping to move constraints out to sales and marketing, in the form of needing more orders to keep everything running at capacity. Me helping to generate enough additional orders to move the constraints back into production. An ideal way to grow a client's business.

Enough now. I'm overheating just thinking about all the ways to make and save money with sales automation. No, it won't cure the common cold. It won't even motivate someone determined not to try. But sales automation can lift up your sales performance, put your reps on a higher performance plane and reduce administrative expenses—in one fell swoop.

Oh, and by the way, burn that copy of *I Made a Million Dropping My Pen on Ready-to-Sign Contracts*. Instead, try my good friend Warren Wechsler's great book, *The Six Steps to Excellence in Selling*. It's about process. The sales process.[9]

---

[9] Warren Wechsler, *The Six Steps to Excellence in Selling* (Minneapolis: Better Books, 1995).

SERVICE OPPORTUNITIES

In most organizations, customer service is much further along the technology curve than either sales or marketing. Does that mean there's less that sales automation can do for service than for sales and marketing? Yes and no.

Sales automation has less to offer customer service per se than it offers the other two disciplines, especially since sales automation *software* is less-than-ideally configured for customer service applications. It's also true that customer service in some industries (the airline industry for example) has little intersection with sales. But the broader-than-software *concept* of sales automation would have a gaping hole if customer service were not involved. After all, how do you effectively marry all of your customer information if you leave out some of the most important interactions with customers we have? How can you build strong customer relationships if relationship builders don't know when their customers are having problems? Pretty hard.

The major customer service opportunities from sales automation involve sharing information between sales and service, often on a real-time basis. Theoretically, we can accomplish that by building links between customer service and sales automation software. But the databases used are often so dissimilar that the inherent difficulty in forging these links deters organizations from trying. Besides, customer service usually lives in operations' or accounting's domain, not sales' or marketing's, and shifting their system allegiance over to sales and marketing is often viewed by operations as a precursor to changing their reporting responsibility to the "revenue" side. For many, that's hard to swallow, no matter how great the benefits to the enterprise.

However, before accepting the "can't do it," "won't fly internally," "more pain than gain" view of tying sales and service data together, reflect on the benefits of:

- *Informing sales* immediately about service issues, so they can intervene in the situation and do some timely hand-holding.

- *Building customer loyalty* through service issues, rather than having it erode.

- *The relative costs of keeping customers,* which most marketing pundits used to project at 25% of the cost of replacing them. Many marketing thought-leaders now peg the percentage at 10% of the replacement cost, or even lower.

- *The sense of "one company"* projected by integrating sales and service data, which sends a powerful message to customers that "we've got out our act together."

And think further, on the expense side of the ledger, about:

- *Service understanding what commitments sales has made,* especially in areas such as information systems or process control equipment, where sales may advise clients to expect problems if they don't change already-installed system elements.

- *Service knowing who's in charge on the customer side,* in order to respond proactively (or ask sales to do so) when an individual customer contact employs relationship-breaking tactics or blames the seller for user problems.

But most importantly, linking the system means:

- *Service understands the relative importance of the customer they're dealing with.*

A recent mishap at one of our top 10 mega-banks is a wonderful, or awful, example of the importance of service knowing customer status. A customer of this financial institution—which was already considering the installation of a melded customer information system—walked into a branch bank and asked to co-sign a new car loan for his college-student daughter. He picked up an application, completed it with his daughter, then returned it. The paperwork went to the service area that evaluates loan applications, and the service person rejected the application. End of story? Hardly. The gentleman who walked in to inquire about the loan was a $15 million trust customer. And he didn't say, "Aw shucks" when he got the rejection. He yanked all $15 million out of this financial institution. Instead of presenting "one face" to the customer, this bank was two-faced. And when the customer didn't like one of those faces, he cut off both. *Sayonara.*

This particular financial institution learned from the experience. Following this incident, it proceeded with a melded sales-service system, post-haste. Unfortunately, many organizations would blame such an incident on "fate," rather than inadequate customer information management.

ADD AN ANGRY CUSTOMER TO A CUSTOMER SERVICE SYSTEM THAT DOESN'T COMMUNICATION WITH SALES, AND YOU HAVE A RECIPE FOR DISASTER.

Personally, I'm on the receiving end of sales-service disconnects all the time. A sales representative for a sales automation software package interests me in a new product, then sends me a demo version. I load it up on my "test" computer (the one that I know will crash periodically because of buggy software) and away I go. More often than not, I have to call tech support because "el software" isn't performing as per the documentation. Then it starts. First, I may get refused service because I don't have a registration number, which often doesn't come on demo copies. Then, on occasion, I get treated like an idiot who's clearly (to the customer service rep) some computer novice and not worthy of their time. (I know it's not personal, at least I hope not; customer service people get frustrated, just as customers do.) I've even been charged for calls triggered by errors in documentation, which are commonplace in sales automation software, because customer service doesn't have a clue about my relationship to their company. All this, while I'm evaluating their product for a future sale.

The quality of the service I receive—if I don't identify myself, or if the service rep doesn't have the latitude to spend a little extra time or "eat" the charges or whatever—can't help but influence my opinion of the product. With a combined sales-service database, service would know that I might be evaluating their program for a potential high-license-volume purchase. No small matter.

One more aspect of melding sales and service data merits your attention. In organizations with a direct (company-employed) field sales force, customer service agents often "adopt" salespeople and do everything possible to help them, sharing information they've received over the phone with "their" reps. It's a wonderful thing to see. Maintaining two unlinked customer databases—one for sales and one for service—makes this type of cooperative communication difficult to maintain. And that frustrates customer service representatives. And frustration leads to turnover, a hideously expensive problem for business.

Integrating sales and service customer data empowers customer service representatives to accomplish much more than patiently taking a pounding at the hands (or mouths) of irritated customers. A well-integrated customer information program does double-duty as an employee retention program by improving customer service morale. Not to mention that it's awfully tough for service reps to leave for another company with inferior customer information management facilities, especially in technology. Think about that.

MARKETING OPPORTUNITIES

Don Peppers and Martha Rogers already wrote the book on marketing opportunities. It's called *The One To One Future*.[10] They followed it up with another excellent book, *Enterprise One To One*.[11] Jill Griffin adds to the literature with *Customer Loyalty*.[12] These and other excellent tomes have primed us for information-driven, customer-based marketing.

Primed us, maybe, but that dang pump still ain't working as often as it should.

And for a good reason. We've been missing a critical tool we need to get closer and stay closer to customers. We've been missing sales automation, particularly enterprise sales automation. Now we have it. Or at least we can have it, if we're committed enough. Reality is starting to catch up with theory, practicality with possibility.

As you read down the list of marketing opportunities, you'll wince just thinking about how *unwelcome* many of these opportunities will be to marketers. Not to all marketers, but unwelcome to media mavens unable to discriminate between marketing and media advertising; unwelcome to creative types who can't imagine how a salesperson could write a letter to a select group of customers that would yield more sales than their award-winning ad or direct mail piece; unwelcome to direct marketers who can't imagine that something else is the future of marketing.

So catch your breath, here comes that list of "opportunities."

---

[10] Don Peppers and Martha Rogers, *The One to One Future: Building Relationships One Customer at a Time* (New York: Doubleday, 1993).

[11] Don Peppers and Martha Rogers, *Enterprise One To One* (New York: Doubleday, 1997).

[12] Jill Griffin, *Customer Loyalty*, (New York: Lexington Books, 1995).

Less media advertising

Placing less reliance on media advertising is a very big marketing opportunity. Think about media advertising's inherent inefficiency, its impersonal manner, its dependency on "one message suits all" creative, its ambient noise level that drives customers crazy. Advertising is an excellent example of how less could be more. Less money spent on advertising, more money to spend on more productive marketing methods. Less emphasis on advertising, more attention paid to information-driven interaction with customers. Heck, marketing could regain a good measure of the respectability it's lost just by listening to customers rather than presuming to know what's best for them. Advertising—it's like a marketing head with the ears chopped off.

Sales automation, in contrast, is about ears. It's all ears, big memory and the capability to process and act on what it hears. Because sales automation listens so well, we can "whisper" the right messages back to customers. Rather than screaming a generic message to the world.

That translates as less direct mail

Yeah, I've dumped more than a few pieces of junk mail in most of your mailboxes. But I'm reforming. Direct marketers keep saying that "there's no junk mail, just misdirected mail, and we're constantly learning more about our customers and what they want to receive." "Ya, sure." And when I open our mailbox I slap my knee and say, "You betcha."

Direct marketers sneak around to get information—from credit files, credit card records, census data, tax files, telephone books, driver licenses, fishing licenses, magazine subscriptions, trade show registrations, birth certificates, garbage cans, you name it. But they're afraid to ask you for it. They're unwilling to let you decide what you want them to know. If they did, they couldn't mail five gazillion pieces of direct mail a year, call you during dinnertime seventeen times a week, fax you stuff you could care less about, and now even litter your e-mail box. And then some presses would grind to a halt. So would some mega-computers. Some phone banks would fall silent. Some trees would be left standing. Dinners would be eaten hot. And long-suffering "targets" of direct mail would dance in the streets.

Less spending

Dare we say it? Look at how much automakers spend on advertising for new customers and how little they spend to keep the ones they have. A sales automation system can track current customers according to their tastes, their preferences, how long they typically keep a car or when their lease ends—what a repeat sales opportunity. Add to that tracking customers who "came close" but bought another make; imagine how fertile that marketing ground is, especially if customer experience with that other make is less than fully satisfactory.

And I'd be remiss not to mention that turnover costs caused by the extraordinary high migration rate of car salespeople would come down if car reps lost their customer databases every time they moved.

Less customer churn

Having a stable, happy customer base helps marketing every bit as much as it helps sales. Happy customers who share their good experience with other customers is among the most powerful marketing tools, perhaps the most powerful.

More business from current customers

Effective customer development eases the pressure of constant new-customer acquisition. That allows marketers to step back and think and work strategically, rather than being in a constant flurry of activity trying to bolster this quarter's numbers.

Less obsession with "brand"

Here we go. More blasphemy. At least to some die-hard believers in mass marketing. But letting sales automation help us get off the brand kick is a huge opportunity.

Look at it this way, brand strength is the next best thing to having a knowledge-based relationship with a customer. But it's a distant second to a relationship. Brand barely appears on the "impact-on-customers" radar screen—except in marketing environments where maintaining individual customer relationships is economically impractical, like household commodities. For packaged goods marketers, fine. They need to rely on brand strength. But for automobile marketers, appliance marketers, computer manufacturers, capital goods manufacturers, most consumer and business service marketers—brand strength can't compete with customer information-driven relationship building for impact on customers. And all this talk about "building customer relationships with a brand"? People are passionate about other people and ideas and even art, but not about advertising constructs like "brand." Let's leave relationships for human interaction.

TRYING TO GET CUSTOMERS TO FORM A "RELATIONSHIP" WITH A BRAND IS LIKE ASKING THEM TO HUG A TELEPHONE POLE.

Hey, add this all up and you have a sales automation bonanza waiting for you. *All you have to do is run the gauntlet to get there.* No sweat.

MANAGEMENT OPPORTUNITIES

Aside from improving the overall well-being of the company, can sales automation affect performance of senior management? *Certainment.*

With very few exceptions, senior management operates at arm's length from customers at best, and often in total isolation from customers. So when senior executives announce a corporate commitment to "customer intimacy," what are the chances they know what they're talking about? Slim to none.

Among the most disappointing sales automation experiences I've had was with an internationally recognized manufacturer. The CEO preached customer intimacy. He even nurtured development of sales automation. But the project had to maintain low altitude in order to avoid hostile fire from several corporate fiefdoms that considered themselves sufficiently autonomous to reject any efforts to "mess with their data." They turned a deaf ear to suggestions that they subordinate their divisional interests to benefit the enterprise.

If you're quicker than I am, which many are, you've realized already that this "nurturing" CEO was the very reason this program had to fly low. He didn't *lead.* Trying to build consensus around cross-divisional data integration can take years, if it can be achieved at all. Enterprise sales automation just doesn't happen without the proactive and ever-present backing and protection of senior management.

Is that a violation of good management policies, to get out front like that? Some of us call it "leadership." Unfortunately, many senior executives don't understand that you get buy-in for *how* you're going to get closer to customers, not *whether* you're going to do so.

Anyway, no sooner did this project appear on-screen than heavy flak burst out. It stayed airborne for a while. Then it took a couple of direct political hits and crashed like a plane straight out of a World War II movie.

So you get up and dust yourself off, knowing that you're going to win some and lose some. Better to be in my position than be one of the prime movers internally.

Had this CEO been in better touch with customers, had his senior managers been in better touch with customers, had they appreciated sales needs (field sales was busily automating itself around ICMs and even a few GCM networks), had they…, had they…, had they…, they would have been smart enough and sensitive enough to understand how much integrated information systems could mean to customers in their industry. Instead, from what I understand through some automation trade talk, the company's primary competitor is about to beat them to the punch and reap the rewards.

TOTAL RELIANCE ON CONSENSUS MANAGEMENT WILL STOP ENTERPRISE SALES AUTOMATION DEAD IN ITS TRACKS.

And how does sales automation put senior management in better touch with customers? Two ways.

Directly, by putting a sales automation station on every senior manager's desktop computer. Not for spying or snooping, but so they can read some call reports, feel the pulse of the market, hear what customers are saying verbatim, view the issues management section of the program and learn customer concerns, directly. Altogether, that's powerful learning, and an opportunity to understand what customer intimacy *should* mean, as opposed to shoving our hand deeper into the customer's pocket.

Indirectly, sales automation can bring each level of management closer to customers. Getting field managers in better touch with customers and with sales has a domino effect. The more the management layer below "gets it," the more the layer above does too, and so on up the ladder. Sales automation has a powerful potential to shorten the distance from customers to senior management. And that's powerful stuff, especially when you consider how many business strategies we base on quantitative, "management decision system" data that's totally devoid of input from the most important and powerful people in any business—the customers.

Oh, and let's not forget. Improving the overall well-being of the company doesn't do senior management any harm, either.

THE BIG LIE

NO, IT'S NOT DATABASE MARKETING

Three things are more likely to screw up a sales force automation than anything else. Confusing it with software is *numero uno*. Failing to garner *proactive* top management support is number two. And confusing sales automation with database or direct or whatever-the-heck-we-want-to-call-it marketing is a very important third. Sure, sales automation strategies often incorporate direct mail, telemarketing and other forms of direct marketing communication. But sales automation is so much bigger than that. And so much better. Even if we only consider the information management aspects, forgetting about the impact on human behavior (although the two are closely intertwined).

In information management terms, sales automation becomes the heart of a complex customer information system. That system pipes customer data from points of customer contact back to a central gathering point, combines contact data with all manner of other data about customers and the things that interest them, melds that data into a well-structured and highly accessible database, then ships appropriate and relevant data back to customer relationship managers and other customer information users (even customers themselves in some circumstances). The importance of direct mail and telemarketing pales in comparison.

But we persist in loading names from (direct) marketing databases onto sales automation software, for use by customer relationship managers as "sales leads," and calling that "sales automation."

Of all the possible sales automation functions, using it to download names of potential customers from corporate to the field is among the least value-producing. Which begs the question, *why do we keep doing this?*

Partly, because we're human. We all share a human tendency to slot new things into familiar reference frameworks. Among all the marketing truths I've tried to impart to the graduate students in my database marketing and micro-marketing courses, the tendency of customers to "slot" a new product category into an established brain compartment ranks right at the top in importance. That's how we understand something new, by comparing it to what we know. And, in a very real way, you are a "customer" evaluating this peculiar new purchase category called "sales automation." So what are you most likely to compare (and confuse) it with? Database marketing, the computer component of direct marketing, which most of us know or have at least a passing acquaintance with.

But there's more to it than just the way we think. There's a huge industry out there —direct/database marketing—which is anxious to lay claim to sales automation as their own new wrinkle. A tactic trying to own a strategy. At trade conferences, in trade publications, in trade meetings, in all of the places we learn about what's new and what's happening in marketing (as opposed to sales), direct marketers are misrepresenting sales automation as a component of their craft; a by-product of their industry, a part of their revenues (which they try to inflate more than advertising inflates its revenues, to see who's top dog in the income race).

That's the big lie.

It took me an embarrassingly long time to understand why the direct marketing industry so persistently scales down sales automation to fit its tool boxes. But finally, I got it. I was attending a National Center for Database Marketing conference in Orlando when I had my own, personal epiphany. Or, better stated, the devil appeared and flashed his horns before me.

Let's replay some of the low lights of this conference— which were "low" enough to sneak under my thick skull and produce a blinding flash of the obvious. In my defense, "the obvious" is often what's most difficult to see, especially when folks are trying to get you to see otherwise.

DELIBERATELY MISLEADING

'Tis always a pleasure to skip out of ice-box-cold Minnesota in winter for points south. So I was looking forward to attending a semi-annual National Center for Database Marketing conference in Orlando, in December. (No, I didn't bring my fishing gear, but I should have.) The meeting's sponsors, the national Direct Marketing Association and Cowles Media, bill this event as a twice-yearly summit of the database marketing industry. Nonetheless, I had waited three years to go again. That seemed about the right interval, to avoid seeing and hearing the same things as before, given the relatively slow rate of change in the database marketing biz.

Now, I admit that I let my expectations rise a little high. But not without reason. The scheduled keynote speakers were Don Peppers and Martha Rogers. The closing-day general session featured Clifford Stoll of *Silicon Snake Oil* fame, a harsh critic of substituting computer "relationships" with personal ones.[13] Both "one to one marketing," which Peppers and Rogers espouse, and building personal buyer-seller relationships are part of my belief system, and have been since the early 1980s, when I switched over from sales to marketing. So Orlando seemed like the right place to be. Especially in December 1996.

Beyond the featured speakers and the normal multiple tracks of normally boring sessions, the conference also offered a day of preconference intensives that caught my attention. Hey, these sessions might provide an opportunity to explore linkages between the new breed of contact-level, relationship management data systems that I had started working with and the traditional, corporate-level marketing databases that are a significant part of my past. Plus, there was a "Software Demo Showcase," always an attraction for a latent propeller-head like me.

---

[13] Clifford Stoll, *Silicon Snake Oil: Second Thoughts on the Information Highway* (New York: Anchor Books, 1995).

And beyond the specific events, there was change. That's what really motivated me to go, aside from the weather. In the three years since I last attended this conference, the field of applying customer information to aid and abet the marketing process had undergone a metamorphosis. Fueled by an explosion in the potential of desktop and laptop software, augmented by a "power surge" in desktop and laptop computers, the role of customer information in the overall marketing process had widened and deepened. Among the incipient changes were a shift from corporate use of marketing data to field use of customer data; a related shift from indirect and inferred knowledge of customers to direct knowledge captured at the point of customer contact; a transition from using information to support centralized direct mail and telemarketing programs to applying information at the point of customer contact to build relationships; and the early stirrings of acceptance of sales, service and marketing as interrelated processes.

I was interested in seeing how the database marketing industry would address change. I actually expected that the conference would address such exciting developments as:

Customer information becoming the ultimate competitive weapon—especially for organizations marketing to high-life-time-value (HLTV) customers. With product parity becoming more the rule than the exception, even in high technology and capital goods markets, managing customer information was on its way to becoming the critical point of distinction that separates winners from losers…in much the same way that product superiority once determined success. Much more exciting stuff than fine-tuning mailing list scoring techniques, which are becoming decreasingly relevant outside of high-volume, low-margin markets, as we enter the age of individual customer marketing; techniques previously, and to my chagrin, still dominant conference fare.

Sales automation arriving full force—and along with it, new, more personal methods of marketing to valuable customers. Laptop computers and sales automation software were already empowering us to collect customer information directly from HLTV customers, to organize and store it locally for contact level-use and to ship relevant portions of it up to the corporate level for management decision-making—all with amazing ease. Quite a turnaround, considering that until recently virtually all customer data had been assembled, processed and stored at the corporate level, then doled out sparingly to field operatives.

Customer marketing (or one-to-one marketing, if you prefer) was becoming a reality—and not a Peppers and Rogers prediction (although their prediction is absolutely contributing to the reality). Mass customization had reached the bicycle market and was rife in capital goods markets. And product development steered by direct customer input, rather than product management projections, was already on the horizon. What an opportunity for everyone involved in customer information management!

Distributed data had finally arrived—better late than never. Marketing was years behind other disciplines in intelligently deploying data at appropriate levels. The marketing data gurus were constrained by fear of data misuse by generalists untrained in database marketing, not to mention the "lepers" (my quotes) in field sales who would be the subject of more than a few disparaging remarks from presenters in Orlando. Can't be trusted with data. Never cooperate. Won't give up their data. The same sales stereotypes that customer-contact-level database developers have disproved and discredited were still alive and well in Orlando. As it happened, attendees did raise questions regarding how to work effectively with field sales in customer data collection and management. But their questions—even insistent questions—were waved off.

Customer knowledge management was on the horizon—and the opportunity to know our customers, rather than just knowing tangential facts about them, was coming into reach.

So what's my problem? You don't have to be a particularly sensitive reader to hear the steam hissing out of my ears. You probably suspect that the Orlando conference really stuck in my craw. You're right. I felt like Andy Rooney on a really bad day. You may also suspect that I went to the wrong conference, that I really didn't belong there. But how could that be? I'm a longtime believer in relationship marketing, as I call Peppers and Rogers' "one to one" philosophy. I share Stoll's fear of loss of customer intimacy on the Internet, if we misuse the medium. And after all, I'm still, literally, a database marketer, no?

But I sure didn't belong in most of the sessions I attended. On the "preconference" first day, the first intensive session I attended turned out to be a history lesson. The speaker acknowledged that his slides were "several years old." They must have been, because they were filled with the names of "dead soldier" companies already buried by change, and even included (by the speaker's admission) dead or dying service categories obviated by market changes.

Also during this session, that nasty issue of sales involvement in "database marketing" emerged from the audience, only to get sidestepped several times. I couldn't stop asking myself, "How can an 'expert' in database marketing ignore the growing realization that sales and marketing are joined at the hip? What was this guy, retro?"

After the session, during which I contributed several polite remarks about different approaches used in building customer databases versus marketing databases, the marketing director for one of this country's better-known financial service providers followed me out of the room. He was fuming. He cornered me and asked why this conference and its presenters "didn't get it" in terms of salespeople being a critical part of the

new equation. I answered as best I could, but what was going
down at this conference still hadn't hit me.

I attended an afternoon intensive session that was more of
the same. This speaker waved off the burgeoning customer data
and relationship management movement as a blip on the
screen—just another source of data to be rolled up into the traditional direct mail database. Yeah, he made the obligatory
references to needing to get beyond a myopic focus on what he termed "centers of tactical excellence." But he then spent the remaining two and a half hours of his session on traditional database seg-mentation within the familiar old direct mail context. I wanted to ask this new ver-sion of the morning's

**DATABASE MARKETING
IS ABOUT JUST THREE
THINGS: DIRECT MAIL
AND TELEMARKETING
— AND COMPUTER
SUPPORT FOR BOTH.**

presenter, "Where have you been, in hibernation?" What
restraint on my part, eh?

Day two, the first full day of the conference, got off to a
much better start. Peppers and Rogers spoke. Not that I believe
they walk on water. In fact, I used to jokingly tell my students
that the authors of *The One to One Future* must have been breathing ether when they wrote the last several chapters; that's how
hypothetical the content gets. But together, they have clearly
identified, articulated and helped bring about the major trend
in marketing today and tomorrow: *we're rapidly moving to an era
of interactive relationships with customers.* Much less stuffing their
mailboxes with junk and calling them at home during dinner
hour, much more laying in the plumbing to bring their voice
back to us marketers. Much less talking. Much more listening.
And Peppers and Rogers are excellent presenters.

Yeah, but even their presentation was troubling. Troubling because they were introduced as part of the database marketing family and symbolic of the conference. In fact, their presentation was antithetical to virtually everything else I saw and heard at the conference, except for Stoll and the attendees who kept asking questions and not getting answers. Questions about the role and importance of contact-level data, the role of sales and the like.

After proclaiming from their podiums that most everything I'd witnessed in the preconference sessions and most everything I would witness in subsequent sessions was off-base, Peppers and Rogers got a thunderous round of applause. Hey, some people hear what they want to hear. Make that lots of people.

But as the conference wore on, it became more and more apparent that a lot of other folks who listened were turned off by most of what they heard. The conference was supposed to be about the future. What it was really about was the past. I saw inordinate numbers of attendees leaving sessions early, with distressed expressions on their faces. Caught some grumblings like, "Just the same old stuff." "Who picked that panel?" "Why won't they address sales issues?" And best of all, "Would somebody tell that joker there's more to life than house file, merge-purge; house file, merge-purge."

But the madness from the podium continued.

"There's one thing we have to understand, you can't trust customers, they lie." "We already have too much customer information." "You can't start a database with customer information, you have to define your segments first." "You should spend at least *two hours* with a client before designing their sales automation database." "We have an interactive dialog with our customers once a month [a credit card marketer referring to their statement]." But the capper for me was a rhetorical question "asked" by one presenter: "This Peppers and Roger stuff is fine, but does anyone here really market one to one?" I raised my hand, eager to debate, ignoring the rhetorical question bit. But he ignored me and continued, "No, of course you don't, it's impractical, so let's talk about customers in segments of at least a thousand." I got up and left. Better than dismembering this clown, limb by limb (verbally, of course).

In fact, the only remaining point of interest for me (at least in the positive sense) was Stoll's presentation. Without my glasses, I could mistake this guy for Robin Williams. Stoll provided some comic relief for an otherwise dreary event. He was focusing primarily on the Internet, but virtually everything he expressed concern over applied equally to traditional database marketing. Reducing customers to a name, a customer number, a segmentation code and a mishmash of inferred or applied data (in other words, educated guesses) inhibits, rather than fosters, customer dialog and customer intimacy.

Stoll, too, received enthusiastic applause. Must have been for his humor.

Gee, what happened? As disheartening as the content of the conference turned out to be, the conference dynamics were worse. From a distance you could mistake the dichotomy between the views of the featured speakers and those of the conference presenters for accommodating, "big tent" stuff. And you could write off the probing questions of attendees that went ignored, because that's not what this conference wanted to be about. But not if you were there, you couldn't. This conference wanted to publicly embrace Peppers and Rogers' one-to-one approach to marketing, bask in its positive image in the business media and business world and, of course, lay claim to it as part of "database marketing."

But inside the sessions—where the real conference took place—the talk was of segmentation, scoring and mass number crunching, and how to improve direct mail results and justify *even more* direct mail. All "what" data and no "why" knowledge. The opposite stuff from the appearance created by hosting these speakers, and contrary to the image the conference tried to portray in its self-promotion.

I'm truly embarrassed to confess how long it took me to "get it." But I've talked to others with database marketing backgrounds similar to mine who also persisted in trying to connect what they did then, direct marketing, with what they do now, sales automation—until they experienced their own blinding flash of the obvious.

On the morning of the third and last day, while I was sitting and stewing over a coffee, somebody turned the light on. I felt like a jerk.

What in hell was I expecting? The database marketing industry doesn't *want* to change. It can't afford to. Sure it wants to look current, but…

The "database marketing complex." Something in the conference triggered distant memories of the stir Dwight Eisenhower made with his parting speech as President—the one where he took on the "military-industrial complex," warning us that we could not and should not determine defense policy by the machinery and skills we have in place to build armaments. That was the cart leading the horse. Instead, Ike had maintained, we must adapt our skills and machinery to meet our needs. Okay, I was in junior high school at the time, but my folks talked a lot about politics, and I overheard this stuff.

Ike's analogy about production capacity driving solutions applied directly to the database marketing industry. Applies even more today.

This industry is hugely vested in the machinery and skills required to pump out high-volume direct mail and huge numbers of telemarketing calls—as productively as machines will allow. But this big machinery doesn't work well for acquiring and managing customer data at the customer contact level. For that matter, it doesn't work at all. Same for the human skills.

The ears lose their sensitivity if you spend much time hugging web presses and machine inserters.

It occurred to me later (much later than it might have occurred to other people) that I was actually in the process of totally retooling myself—new tool box, new skill set, new everything. I'd left the agency business, and for the most part left database marketing, because I was spending the majority of my time doing the wrong things the wrong way—because I couldn't figure out how to practice the personal-level marketing I believed in while trapped in an agency environment, using traditional database marketing skills.

THE DATABASE MARKETING INDUSTRY HAS A HUGE INVESTMENT IN FIXED ASSETS, WHICH IT HAS TO PAY OFF.

So *that's* what I was doing, on my own, in the relationship marketing and sales automation consulting business. Duh.

But back to the conference. Instead of focusing on change, the conference had concerned itself with, *how do we utilize our existing capacity?* This conference was all about preserving a role for our present inventory of machinery and skills. It was, in that sense, a conference dedicated to resisting change, or slowing it down. Not a conference about embracing or even accepting change. Change was not an option.

Information-based marketing had divided into two industries: "database communication" and "relationship management." From a subject-matter standpoint, the conference made several forays beyond providing computer support for direct mail and tele-marketing applications. But these came across as tokenism, as attempts to lay claim to the changes that are fast overtaking the traditional database marketing industry. "Hey Dick, wake up. You're in competition with these guys." Sales automation is competing with database marketing for share of budget dollars, for share of jobs, for share of stature.

In a very ironic way, the competition resembles the age-old tug-of-war between database marketing and advertising. Database marketing made a lot of hay over claims that it was more personal, more customer-friendly than advertising. So guess what. Here I am writing about database marketing from the sales automation perspective, just as database marketers wrote about advertising. The shoe is now on the other foot. What goes around comes around. Whatever. Guess that shows we all live in glass houses. Hope I haven't thrown too many big stones.

No big surprise, in hindsight, that relationship marketing and sales automation don't mix with database marketing in one conference. Peppers and Rogers didn't belong at this conference. Nor did Stoll. Nor did a considerable number of people who attended.

In fact, we have two database-related marketing movements: traditional, communication-oriented database marketing on one hand; and the new relationship marketing of Peppers and Rogers and contact-level data and sales automation on the other. The direct mail and telemarketing

DATABASE MARKETING AND SALES AUTOMATION ARE LOCKED IN COMPETITION OVER PRIORITY AND BUDGET.

folks, including the database specialists who support them, already "own" the database marketing name. Which makes me no longer a "database marketer." Which makes "database" conferences like this one irrelevant to me.

They can have the moniker. They can have their conferences. But it really annoys me that they wave Peppers and Rogers in front of the marketing industry and say, "That's us."

No, that's not you. Not even close.

But let's not end on a sour note. While my initial reaction to the conference was disappointment with the content and anger over the deception, the lasting impact was wonderfully positive.

Sometimes, the best way to learn what something is, is to learn what it's not. My own attempts to find continuity between relationship marketing and sales automation, where I live today, and database marketing, where I lived for many years, was coloring my view of sales automation. Among the lessons I took from Orlando was that I had not simply sauntered from one "room" in the marketing house to the next; instead, I had gone somewhere outside the traditional marketing realm. Now I was part marketing strategist, part sales system developer, part trainer, part propeller-head and part organizational development consultant (at least to the point of sniffing out problems before the fact, and knowing that enterprise sales automation clients were about to make changes that extend far beyond sales and marketing). And that's a very rich place to be in terms of personal satisfaction. In no traditional marketing or sales position do you have the opportunity to accomplish so much, or the responsibility to help so much.

I've always been an interdisciplinary consultant, one who would tell a client to put their marketing wallet away and invest in removing an impediment to marketing first. But I've always operated within marketing confines. What I learned in Orlando is that those ties that bound were gone. Doing sales automation *right,* especially enterprise sales automation, requires a lot more than wearing a marketing hat with a sales visor. It requires multiple hats, and affords rewarding opportunities to work with peers who wear those other hats full-time. It also requires working very close to the spine of the organization, rather than on appendages, which sales and marketing have unfortunately become.

Database marketing may be locked in a tactical world of direct mail and telemarketing communication and fancy databases to support them, but thankfully, sales automation is not. And don't let anyone tell you otherwise.

By the way, I just got the flyer for the next conference. Same fare (but no Peppers and Rogers or Stoll). Orlando again, too. Or should we call it Disney World.

There. I've had my say.

Looking back on what I just wrote, I expect my e-mail's going to be just a 'hummin' with responses from died-in-the-wool database types. Even some old friends and clients. Reminds me of the reaction to a journal article I wrote a few years back about paying more attention to doing customer marketing than seeing who could brand everybody's work with their consultancy's particular

HOPEFULLY, YOU'LL NEVER BE TEMPTED TO CONFUSE SALES AUTOMATION WITH DATABASE MARKETING, NO MATTER WHO TRIES TO CONFUSE YOU AND HOW HARD THEY TRY.

moniker. One of the "IMC" (integrated marketing communications) guys threw a rod. Could smell the bearings burning long-distance. Told the magazine he'd never write for them again. Still hasn't.

So hey, maybe some database marketers will get so mad they refuse to write at all, magazine or book. Free up some shelf space for this puppy. We'll see how it goes. But I've got my helmet on, just in case.

Switching Gears

Take a deep breath. Take a break. Take a walk. But don't take a hike. We're not done yet. But when you return, you'll return to a different book. No more "philosophy of marketing" (okay, you know I'll lapse a little). No more big picture. No more global stuff. IT'S MEAT AND POTATOES TIME! Hope you're hungry.

So far, we've talked the talk. Now we're going to do you know what. And I'll try to keep it from getting too pedestrian. But you gotta know how to do this stuff. So roll up your sleeves, take a few of the pain relievers of your choice, and get ready to wallow in the dirty details.

To tell the truth, I love this part. Some of my colleagues think I'm a little strange, that way.

"Geez, get someone else to do that for you."

"Why are you wasting your time on implementation."

"Have the software guys do that."

The software guys? We're not even close to software yet. In fact, all we've done is talk. Now we're going to "do." So strap on your seat belt one more time. Only this time, you don't get to take it off until the very end. Sorry.

II.
DEPLOYING SALES AUTOMATION

PHASE I

SALES AUTOMATION DEPLOYMENT MAP

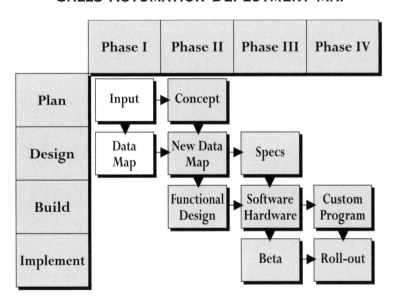

	Phase I	Phase II	Phase III	Phase IV
Plan	Input →	Concept		
Design	Data Map	New Data Map →	Specs	
Build		Functional Design →	Software Hardware →	Custom Program
Implement			Beta →	Roll-out

Plan your entire sales automation implementation
process before you begin building your system.

DON'T PANIC! It's not going to be that bad, I promise. The same deployment chart for pages and pages. We'll break it down into individual steps. One step after the other, just like walking. You'll be asking for a new chart before we finish this one (hopefully you will, because there are more to come).

Sales automation works the same way lots of other stuff does—like building houses. You can't build a house without a plan, at least not a house you'd want to live in. Same goes for sales automation. You need a complete plan on your desk before you commit to anything other than planning. So here's a good way to go about it.

INPUT

You'd be astonished at how many sales automation projects are designed by a group of corporate managers and nefarious consultants sitting around a corporate conference room with carafes of coffee and a sideboard of Danish. Not a representative from relationship management in sight, often not even a representative from field marketing. But you won't be surprised to hear that most sales automation systems designed by corporate management and consultants, in isolation from the relationship side, fail miserably. *Sales automation is a customer-contact-level activity and information system first, foremost and always.* Try turning sales automation into a conduit for corporate to bulk-ship stuff to field sales in particular, and field sales will almost certainly turn their backs on it. Try to extract stuff from sales and service without giving them what they want from sales automation—the "top-down" approach—and they'll walk away from it. Try to force sales to use it. Good luck.

Get input from relationship managers first

It only stands to reason that relationship managers, the sales and service representatives who use sales automation day-to-day, should be among its primary architects. And while service representatives have little choice but to use the system provided them, not so with sales. If sales automation helps sales sell more with less effort, they'll use it. If it interferes with their selling, they won't. If it's a wash, some will use it but most won't.

That's not to say that you have to listen to sales and service reps, give them only what they want and stop there. Once you've given them what they want, you can ask them for what you want out of sales automation. And you can usually get what you need, if you work hard to delight your relationship managers by providing sales automation features that demonstrate your respect for them and for the difficult jobs they do.

Sales automation should be win-win for relationship managers, line management and corporate management. It's a *quid pro quo* game, although skewed in favor of relationship managers. You give sales a calendar and activity manager conveniently connected to customer records, and they'll ship you their sales activity information via remote synchronization. You give them office automation tools that virtually spit out customer communication and proposals, cut sales forecasting time to a fraction of what they now spend, do likewise to expense reports and enable them to mount local direct mail programs with consummate ease, and they'll invest some of the time you saved them capturing customer perspectives on your brands and products; identifying unmet market needs; obtaining capital equipment replacement schedules, supply inventories and projected materials needs; ferreting out lists of buyers for other reps in the organization…you name it (within reason).

You give, you get. And you get more if you take the time to explain your every step in deploying sales automation to your relationship management team, and do it from a relationship management perspective. But don't try explaining what you're doing after the die is cast. *You have to start the sales automation development process by giving relationship managers a voice in the system design.* Not control, but a voice, and a strong one.

Beyond loving your customers (which most of us now concede we must), you need to love your relationship managers and respect their work before sales automation will work.

Don't forget customer service input

Of those sales automation systems not designed around management needs, too high a percentage still leave customer service out of the loop, literally and figuratively. Here's a tip: you can't backtrack and pick up customer service in phase 2. Service automation needs are so different from sales needs that the software program you select to meet sales needs only is unlikely to support service very well, if at all.

Interestingly, when you talk with customer service, their top priority is often better communication with sales. It's in the self-interest of both to share customer information, especially that friendly "look out" when a customer's back is up. It's also very much in the customers' best interest for sales and service to work in sync.

SALES AND SERVICE CAN'T BE GOOD PARTNERS WITHOUT SHARING CUSTOMER DATA.

Bring customer service into the loop at the beginning of your process—unless customer service and sales have no reason to interact in your environment. And that's rare.

Dealing with "silo management" impulses

Despite all of the recent efforts at changing corporate structures, most organizations are still structured around division and/or departmental silos; i.e., private "turfs" that divisions and departments zealously protect out of self-interest. It just so happens that customer service is frequently a pawn in the turf battles of various competing factions.

The benefits of hooking sales and service together notwithstanding, putting customer service on your sales automation system may not be high on others' agendas. So think twice before you sidle into a management meeting and casually suggest that customer service just "slide over" onto the new system in order to link directly with sales. Some bruiser from accounting might slide over and kneecap you.

Traditionally, customer service has been most often aligned with accounting, rather than sales and marketing. Why? Because in American business, "control" is more important than "customer." Unless they're an unusually customer-focused bunch, accounting will fight hard to keep customer service on the "main" (operations) system where accounting resides. And they have a significant data integration issue on their side.

Sales automation is PC-based. But most large-organization customer service staffs sit at dumb terminals connected to the operations system in general, and to accounting in particular. And switching a customer service department from a mainframe platform over to a PC platform can be expensive. The problem that surfaces in so many corporate meetings addressing the possibility of moving service onto a new sales automation system is financial feasibility—that it's neither practical nor affordable nor in anyone's budget to move customer service reps over to PCs.

There may be truth to this. However, "wrong platform" is often a politically correct way of saying "wrong department." Very often, disputes over which system customer service should work on are really turf battles over which management silo customer service reports through.

Now, before you start thinking I'm operations-averse or accounting-averse, let me put their control-oriented approach into perspective. Operations and financial folks are products of an overall business environment that's long valued internal controls and considerations more than customer information management and customer relationships. Hey, we *can't* recoup money we lost this way or that way, but we *can* replace a customer.

For example, the financial services company where my wife and I invest the bulk of our retirement savings doesn't blink at sending us "disintegrated" statements that make it a chore to figure out the value of our investments. We've heard from their relationship managers that lack of integrated statements costs them share of customer and even whole customers. Still, customer-friendly statements haven't been a high enough priority to get badly needed attention. Good thing they're a client of mine, or they'd be history.

But, before you lay a heavy rap on the operations side, ask yourself this. Are finance, accounting, IT and other operations functions unique in working from an old and now inappropriate set of priorities? Heck no.

What operations functions are doing data-wise is no worse, no worse at all, than what marketers are doing media-wise. I cringe (and hear a flushing sound) when I see much of the business-to-business advertising on television. Wake up, sports fans. Customers aren't watching. And if they are, they're zapping. And if they're not zapping, they'd rather not be transported back to the office during the precious few hours they have to relax.

But media advertising is the "go to" approach for most marketers and has been for decades. Take half a business-to-business media advertising budget and apply it to relationship marketing and customer information management, and the remainder might migrate very soon. I can show many organizations selling all manner of high-ticket or repetitive purchase merchandise how they can increase their marketing ROI by marketing one to one. But it's hard to get most to listen. They're too accustomed to thinking media advertising first, a bias fed by their advertising agencies, which live off media advertising. Change is very hard for marketers to accept. And just look at how hard many sales types have fought computerization and process management.

SENDING MULTIPLE STATEMENTS FOR RELATED PRODUCTS SHOWS A LACK OF CONSIDERATION FOR THE CUSTOMER.

So, before you start labeling accounting, IT and others in your path "intransigent," stop and think about how hard marketing and sales have resisted change. Then, before you try to initiate major changes that may clash with one functional area's value system or another's—like trying to switch customer service data over to a sales automation information system, a precursor to switching customer service over to the sales and marketing side of the tracks—sit down with your potential adversaries and with senior management and discuss the pros and cons. And if the decision goes in your favor, put yourself in the other side's shoes. Sales automation can cause so much shuffling of so many functions that you can't go around starting fires. You're going to need all the energy you can muster to put them out.

In the case of moving customer service data management over to sales automation, be prepared to lose this battle, at least in round one. And if you lose, be careful to lose only the battle, and not your entire sales automation project.

But whatever you do, *don't design customer service "out" of your sales automation system forever by selecting software that won't support service applications, now or later.*

Involve all significant stakeholders

Today, it's a simple sales automation project. Tomorrow, someone from manufacturing drops by and says, "Hey, if sales could combine their proposals and upload weighted counts on projected orders, we could reduce materials inventory and speed up manufacturing lines." Suddenly, you glaze over— and you regret your decision to save a few dollars per user and go with a closed system that can't readily exchange data, or with a contact manager that can't count (several of the best-selling contact managers can't do basic math).

SOME POPULAR SALES AUTOMATION SOFTWARE PACKAGES CAN'T PERFORM BASIC MATH FUNCTIONS, SUCH AS ADDITION AND SUBTRACTION.

That's classic "sales automation migration." Project creep. Happens all the time. The only way to prepare for project creep, which you really want to encourage, is to plan as though every information system in the company may sooner or later connect with your sales automation system. Talk to everyone who might pull data from the system or add data to it. Identify all their potential needs and contributions, and work with IT to understand the system's implications. You don't have to tie everything together now. You just need to design your core system as if you are, because you very likely will.

Another aspect of the issue of integrating disparate systems and platforms is knowing whether a link is under construction somewhere out in that wacky world of software development. I spend lots of time with my ear to the ground listening for rumblings of new integration links under construction or even under consideration. Already we have Open Database Connectivity (ODBC) standards that more and more software developers are adhering to. Several years from now, cross-platform data transfer (such as *readily* moving accounting data on a UNIX system to sales automation on a Windows system) may be a problem of the past. Before you assume that some manner of data integration is impossible, or accept that conclusion from someone else, listen and ask around.

Separate individual or group agendas from facts

When you interview everyone and their cousin in the company regarding their potential involvement with sales automation and sales automation data, you'll certainly hear some axes grinding. "I won't do this." "They can't do that." "Marketing is out to get us." "Sales is too lazy to do any of this." Etc.

You can't afford to have grudges and negative perspectives dictate your system design. An effective way to guard against this problem is to interview people in cross-functional groups.

Get representatives from sales, marketing, IT, accounting, product management and elsewhere into one room. It's amazing how much petty stuff goes away when the objects of criticism are within earshot. Also, write up meeting reports and circulate them to everyone attending and everyone concerned.

I recently had a meeting with a multifunction group from a new client to discuss integration issues. Until then, IT had been reluctant to consider anything other than building the system in-house. Ten minutes into the meeting I discovered that IT was unaware of anything other than shrink-wrapped sales automation programs that perhaps allowed some customization by a third-party VAR. When IT learned about the new breed of relationship management systems with their flexibility and extensive user-customization options, the issue was defused. Doubly so when they looked at the very process map we're working from here and saw "software selection" after all the system specs were written.

That's what an open, informational meeting can do.

On the flip side, though, take care to hear out key people with serious concerns in private, preferably before you start bringing groups together. That way, you can put into play legitimate reservations that people may be afraid to bring up for fear of retribution (you, of course, are unafraid). Silence can be just as pernicious as raging personal agendas in a group buy-in process.

When in doubt, validate

During your interviews, you're also likely to hear some improbable stuff. "This database can't talk to that one." "You can't import into this database; all data has to be manually keyed in." "We need our data this way, and there's no flexibility." "We can't invoice properly this way."

Often (but not always), it's bunk. If you need it done, but someone says it can't be done, get a second opinion. Ask why and bounce it off someone else. Call in an outside consultant.

Just the threat of doing so can loosen up the truth before you ever pick up the phone.

In today's information-rich business environment, *there are no excuses for building closed systems, only ulterior motives.* If data really can't be moved in and out of an application or legacy system, it's time for a new system. Few organizations will be able to compete for very long without effective information sharing, particularly sharing of customer information.

Above all, persist. Too many work-arounds will kill a sales automation project. And if you let one department or functional area screw things up, be prepared to let everyone do it. Every person you deal with reports to someone higher, someone who's supposed to see the forest not the trees. If someone stands in the way of sales automation and melding of customer information, despite reason or evidence indicating they can afford to be more flexible and cooperative, take your reason or evidence up the ladder. Better yet, have whoever placed the responsibility for sales automation in your lap go with you.

Don't abdicate responsibility for sales automation to IT

Not that they necessarily want it. But some IT departments do see sales automation as systems work, just as many marketers and sales managers mistake it for software. Sales automation requires extensive systems work. It requires specialized software. But, *sales automation is a fundamental re-engineering of sales and marketing processes.* That's human work. Sure it requires systems work and software, but *no one except sales and marketing, with participation and support from senior management, can successfully re-engineer sales and marketing processes.* Good IT departments and managers see this and respect it. And a friendly IT presence is a godsend to a sales automation project. But a "systems first" or otherwise hostile IT presence can kill SFA dead, beyond revival, if senior management lets it.

An early career experience of mine, long before sales automation came into play, taught me a valuable lesson about working with IT that's served me well over the years. Being a glutton for punishment, I had jumped from BusCo to another "pony express" package express carrier that I'll call Semi-National Courier.

Hey, at least we *flew* the freight instead of stuffing it under busses. But we didn't fly most of it on our own planes, which turned out to be the source of my "opportunity" to be a burr in IT's saddle and the source of my subsequent near-firing.

After experiencing a year-or-so's frustration with our erratic, ad hoc air service to cities not serviced by our air charter network, I decided to take the bull by the horns and negotiate a deal with A Big Airline (ABA), which then serviced virtually every major city we didn't, with flights leaving its hub between 1:00 a.m. and 3:00 a.m.

We would fly our freight to ABA's hub city on flights arriving by midnight, using special "belly loads" that ensured that our freight came off first. Our staff there would consolidate our packages with packages from other Semi-National terminals that could ship to the hub via ABA before midnight. The consolidated shipments, which cost far less to ship than individual packages, were belly-loaded so they went on the appropriate ABA flights at the last possible moment. Everyone in our network would all get faster, more reliable and less expensive service, which we could market like the dickens. Plus, we would finally have near-national air routing to all major points—allowing us to compete with the big boys. Sort of, anyway.

There were only three hitches to this scheme. First, turns out it was barely legal, if at all. Something about Wright-Patman. Both ABA's and Semi-National's attorneys broke out in hives over it. Second, I was regional sales manager for New England at the time, and I lacked any authority to negotiate a deal affecting the whole network with ABA's corporate office in a locale that hardly resembled New England (yes, I did this in winter, and ABA's HQ was someplace warm). Third, Semi-National already had a director of air services at HQ in Minnesota who'd been saying all along that all-points air routing was an impossibility. Nothing major.

When the *generalissimo* of the Semi-National Air Force heard what this impudent you-know-what in Boston had done, he had to scraped off the ceiling. Finally, though, they decided to fly me to the frozen tundra to explain to the Air Tribunal how this would work. Grudgingly, they acknowledged that this *would* work—although no one could figure out how to keep regional managers from pulling freight off of our charter planes, which cost them an arm and a leg because of internal charge-backs, and using the much less expensive line-haul I'd negotiated with ABA.

Anyway, after they flew me to Minnesota, they moved me there, with the charge of computerizing our line-haul air schedules and all of our ground service points, too. Then we would be able to publish a national service guide, like everyone else. So I packed my fishing rods and dutifully came to this wonderland with walleye in the bathtubs and northern pike in backyard swimming pools. You betcha.

I set to working with IT (back then we called it MIS, but I won't and avoid further confusing matters). I tried to cajole the programmers into computerizing the logic I'd used to create Boston's air-routing manual. They were resistant, because it was "inelegant" and too subject to interpretation. But I persisted, until finally the IT team leader threw a report on my desk and said, "This is the best we can do. We have other projects waiting."

So I did the best I could do. As it happens, the reason for my working first at BusCo and then Semi-National Courier was that some very kindly managers were willing to wink at my going off to class at 4 p.m. I was finishing my MBA at Suffolk University in Boston (after spending a dozen years in the rock music industry developing no marketable skills). Although my concentration was marketing, I believed that computers would become vital to marketing and sales, so I started learning my way around the mainframe environment, which was all that existed in those days. And while doing so, I learned to write COBOL, the very code that Semi-National used. So I wrote my own program, walked into the team leader's office, tossed it on his desk and said, "Just run this, and I'll be happy."

Not a particularly endearing thing to do. The head of IT, who was an executive VP and the second-in-command at good old SNC, demanded that I be fired, post haste. One more in a series of kindly managers saved my butt, although not before giving the matter considerable thought. For my penance, I had to submit to letting the VPIT stomp on my head for a very long time. It was worth it, because while he was pretending that I was grass and he was a lawnmower, he conveyed a message that has meant lots to me over the years.

IT'S EASIER TO CREATE COLLISIONS WITH IT THAN TO REPAIR THE DAMAGE ONCE ITS DONE.

After he finished "mowing my yard," he explained that he was so angry because I had embarrassed his staff in a way that was hugely demoralizing, which obligated him to go to bat for them. "Why didn't you come and talk to *me* before you did that?" he asked me. "Why didn't you show that program to me? And why didn't you stick to communicating what you needed instead of starting off trying to tell my staff how to do it?"

He was right. I had screwed up royally. I had made it almost impossible to gain future cooperation. Since then, I've seen a number of SFA projects stuck in their tracks by a tug-of-war, with IT on one side and sales and marketing types on the other. This battle is a constant topic of sales automation talk, because it happens all the damn time.

Oh, and before he finished, he had one last comment. He looked at the sheaf of papers with the hand-written code I'd given his team leader and said, "Good program. I'll get it run in the next couple of days."

The VPIT and I became friends. We even worked together on a consulting project after our SNC days. I ate some crow and developed an effective working relationship with his staff. And getting back on the right foot allowed us to get past some very delicate issues down the road.

It never pays to aggravate people whose support you need, no matter what they do.

Aside from the difference in perspective and priorities, another "sticky wicket" you may have to pass through with IT involves working in a Windows environment. Few corporate IT departments have substantial systems development expertise in a PC/Windows-based environment. That's not what they're paid for. Still, that won't stop some IT folks from seeing sales automation as an intrusion on their turf, and they do have a point. They are paid to supervise all significant data management within the enterprise.

Can you imagine how marketing and sales mangers would feel if IT developed a slick, new automated way to communicate with customers without sales and marketing involvement? Sales and marketing would scream bloody murder. The point here is that sales automation changes the boundary between IT and sales and marketing, and it also requires new skills that IT may not have yet. But managing data is also IT's job, so don't go trucking in there wearing combat boots.

The best way to avoid having a relatively easy systems job on Windows wind up as a very complex job on a mainframe or mini or other non-Windows environment is to *stay off the systems and software issues entirely, until you've finished re-engineering your sales and marketing processes.* Software and systems are essential tools, and you're certainly going to need help from experts in developing and using these tools. But your goal in sales automation is to improve sales and marketing processes, from which flow new customer information strategies. Sales, marketing and senior management have to determine how that's best done. Then, hopefully, the systems and software experts will help determine how best to support it.

Finally…gee, can you tell I'm sensitive to the possibility of things going wrong between sales automation and IT? I'm not sensitive. I'm outright PARANOID. Finally, consider that sales and marketing have largely abdicated responsibility for the process aspect of their functions. Who's lap has this responsibility landed in? IT's. Does it belong there? No. When sales and marketing suddenly show up and attempt to snatch it back, aren't the likely resistance and hard feelings understandable?

Be aware of organizational consequences

As you go around gathering sales automation input, be sensitive to sales automation's potential impact on other functional areas—areas you may regard as tangential players. Ralph Jacobson, of Synthesis Consulting, an organizational development colleague who has helped many organizations work through difficult structural changes, has a favorite saying: "Change the information flow, and you change the company."

> "CHANGE THE INFORMATION FLOW, AND YOU CHANGE THE COMPANY."
> — RALPH JACOBSON

A significant percentage of sales automation projects fail because their consequences on organizational development come as a complete surprise, and no one has made any preparations for dealing with these consequences.

When you sense that your sales automation plans may affect others in ways that aren't immediately apparent, raise a flag and

let people know. It's easier to work through these issues honestly and openly in advance, than risk having the whole project
tumble down around your ears because someone with veto
power got territorial after realizing what was going down.

Okay, so we all cheat on that a little. Just don't cheat on
it a lot.

Find a powerful sponsor (or two or three)…before you start

When "the stuff" does hit the fan because sales automation is
going to affect someone or some department in ways they don't
appreciate—and that *will* happen unless you're only doing a
scratch-the-surface job—you may need political weight on the
sales automation team. In fact, you may need lots of it, unfortunately. If you let it, the political dust that whips up when the
realization sinks in that sales automation is much more than
software can turn into funnel cloud. That's another of the principal reasons that 69.5% of sales automation projects, or
whatever the number is, fail.

In the end, either you have powerful sponsors, or you
become a victim of some "unfortunate accident." Or the project
gets put on hold pending peace negotiations never concluded.
Or the whole project gets sent to committee, where it gets
gummed to death. And the more you experience sales automation migration, which brings more non-sales and marketing
players into the loop, the more you need a mucky-muck or two
or three to step in and save you and the project at critical
moments. Remember, corporations don't hand out Purple
Hearts to loyal employees who suffer political wounds while
trying to do the right thing by their companies. These unintentional martyrs usually get led out to pasture or shown the door.

Protect yourself and your project, but be respectful of others. And keep your sponsors in the loop. When you need them,
you really need them; and they're not much help if you've left
them in the dark about what you're doing and why.

DATA MAPPING

After negotiating the hazards of getting initial input, data mapping should be a real treat. You get to schedule a whole day in the conference room, enjoy endless pots of coffee, have breakfast and lunch catered in, and draw with colored markers. Whooppeeee!!

For some perverse reason, I enjoy data mapping. But it puts some people to sleep and reminds others of a day in the dentist's chair. In fact, a client who happens to be CEO of a high-tech firm, and who's been in the computer game his whole career, said to me, "I hate this stuff. It's too boring. Give me something strategic to think about."

Anyway, here's the drill.

Invite everyone to a big party

Well, not everyone, but make sure you schedule time with everyone who wants to have a say in how sales automation will unfold. And invite any prominent "troublemakers" who believe that sales automation is subordinate to whatever they do, whether they're in sales or marketing or IT or financial services or wherever. When these individuals see everyone's data going up on the wall together, their green boxes don't look any more important than the red or purple ones for other functional areas, even in their own eyes. I've disarmed many a sales automation opponent and even created some important allies at data mapping sessions.

Draw a big picture

Depending on the size and complexity of your organization, you may have to draw several pictures and piece them together at the end of the session, but the point's the same. You can talk data flow to death and still not have a clear picture of what customer data is going where, through what and why. On the other hand, if you draw a big picture of boxes and lines, and label them, it all comes clear. All except the "why" part, which often remains a mystery.

Data mapping is nothing more—or less—than putting down on paper, in very cryptic fashion, all customer data flow within the enterprise. You're best off starting with sales data at points of customer contact and working back from there. Then add marketing data (ignoring third-party data such as mailing lists and demographic, lifestyle and SIC data for the time being). Then add transaction data, then billing and accounts receivable data, then product and manufacturing data that either relationship managers or service staff or *customers* might like to have, and then anything else that is relevant.

Mapping data one function at a time has several benefits. First, you can bring in even more people to get depth of input at a function level, without having them participate in the whole process. Remember, conference rooms are always at the very end of the ventilation line. Second, you can map data elements and flow in order of priority to sales automation, which will help keep you from getting bogged down by tangential issues.

And why, a paragraph ago, did I suggest that you ignore third-party data for the time being? Because, in sales automation terms, most of it isn't worth the magnetic tape it's stored on. It's direct marketing data, and one of the unfortunate influences direct marketing has on sales automation is lowering data quality standards. Unlike mailing lists, which can work very effectively when they're only partially accurate, *sales automation data must be exceptionally accurate*. Remind yourself of the cost difference between sending a direct mail letter to the wrong person, on one hand, and on the other, having a sales representative waste valuable time on a no-potential "prospect." That will help keep you on the straight and narrow in terms of overuse of relatively low-quality direct marketing data.

Here's another, closely related, caveat. Don't consider raw sales inquiries an accurate source of sales automation data. I can speak from long experience, including time spent as a principal of a sales inquiry management business, and say unequivocally that *sales inquiries need prequalification before they go to field sales.* It doesn't matter whether raw inquiries travel to the field on paper, through e-mail or via sales automation database synchronization. Garbage is garbage. Flushing raw sales inquiries down the sales automation pipeline just creates lots of mini-data dumps. You don't want that—really, you don't. By the way, if you hear e-mail mentioned in conjunction with sales automation, be aware that whoever is saying it may very well be thinking about how to lay high-volume pipe for "flushing" purposes.

By all means, however, plan to enter raw sales inquiries in your sales automation system. Doing so will automate the tele-qualification process, making it faster and less expensive. It will also automate the process of sending qualified leads to field sales, complete with full notes from the qualification contact.

Following are two charts that show typical data mapping output. The first one shows a "rough cut" overview. The second shows detail for customer information flowing to and from sales.

While you don't have to gussy up your flow charts to look like these after the actual mapping session, I've found that doing so greatly aids in clearly communicating "what is" and why it has to be changed. That's especially true when you use a keyboard to show manual entry, or put a big black "X" between systems that can't talk to each other. Down the road, creating user-friendly charts will also serve as a good defense against less-than-forthright folks intent on tripping you up. Been there, seen that. With charts like these, it's harder for them to say, "Shucks. I didn't realize what we were considering. I don't read charts very well."

"ROUGH CUT" VIEW

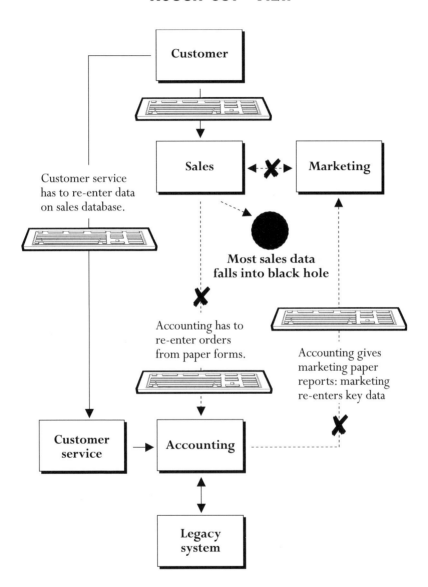

Dotted lines with Xs show where data won't go, at least not electronically. This customer information flow takes care of accounting and no one else, and it even creates extra work for accounting.

DETAIL: DATA FLOW THROUGH SALES

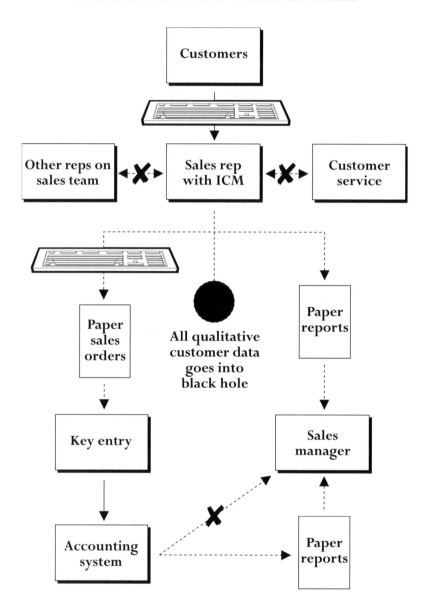

When we isolate on sales, things look even worse.

Micrografx FlowCharter, which I use, is a great program for this purpose. Visio should also work well.

Writing with Invisible Ink

Sound like we're ready to move on? No, no no. We still have to discuss the most important aspect of first-cut data mapping.

You must map all the "phantom" information you should be—but aren't—collecting from and about customers.

In fact, you might schedule a brainstorming meeting or three just to identify all the valuable sources of customer knowledge potentially available to you, both internally and externally. A lot of this will be "why" data that you've never been able to manage before.

How do you map this missing info? Actually, not with invisible ink. Nor with a grease pencil.

Here's how. Draw arrows from the sources of missing information to big "black circles" on your data map. Big as in "you can't overlook them," no way, no how. Then, in the map key, where you identify all the neat stuff like "keyboard stands for second, third or 99th manual re-entry of data that's already been entered once," label these circles "black holes."

When you re-map your data, you want to erase every possible black hole. Converting these black holes into systematic data flows is a critical aspect of sales automation.

PHASE II

SALES AUTOMATION DEPLOYMENT MAP

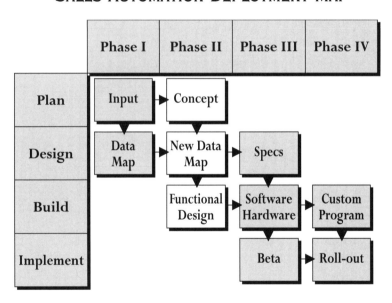

	Phase I	Phase II	Phase III	Phase IV
Plan	Input → Concept			
Design	Data Map	New Data Map → Specs		
Build		Functional Design	Software Hardware → Custom Program	
Implement			Beta → Roll-out	

Phase II is where your project picks up speed and really starts rolling.

Many organizations preparing to implement sales automation already collect lots of customer information—which then disappears into black holes. That's true of both "what" and "why" information. The desire to "put it somewhere" before more is lost can trigger a hasty sales automation software search. Don't worry about losing a little more data, if the price of saving it is a hurried sales automation implementation.

Software vendors are only too happy to feed your fears of losing data and rush to the fore to save you, all declaring that their package is better than the others' for your needs, whatever those needs happen to be, and that competitive software programs X and Y have fatal flaws. Hey, this one system even electrocuted some poor rep.

You're not ready to talk software yet. Not until you've agreed internally on a concept, drawn a new data map to flesh out the concept and then arrived at a functional design that defines what your sales automation software needs are and what they aren't. Bite hard and let the data go for a little while longer. Better that than rushing into a system that won't provide full use of the data after capture.

If any software vendors push you to do otherwise, cross them off your lest. They're selling software, not solutions. And if you get the old line about, "Stick to the sales part, if you worry about all this other stuff you'll never get started," translate that as, "Damnit, I need more sales to make quota or to be top reseller for the year. I don't have time for all this 'thinking.'"

CONCEPT

If you're the impatient type, and hate all this meticulous planning stuff, it's your time now. But only briefly. Before you dive into big-picture thinking, though, think about where you'd be if you hadn't taken the time to attain critical information mass before starting. You'd be where so many organizations wind up on the road to sales automation, trying to take a U-turn to double-back and learn what they missed the first time around. Besides, human nature dictates that most who turn back don't go back far enough to get straightened out. Because who really wants to learn that everything they've done has to be redone? Much better to risk having to turn back again and again and again, no? No.

I recently encountered an organization that typified this attitude. These folks decided on a software package before doing their homework. As a check, they decided to have an IT guy with zero process management experience match their business processes against the software they'd virtually selected. And now they're ready to go. Hope they stay ready, because they're going to go, go again and go another time; hopefully, through luck or process of elimination, they'll eventually stumble across half a solution. How do you tell people you can't get here from there? Write a book, I guess.

Bottom line, *if you skimmed through this book and decided to start reading about implementation, please go back.* If you don't, you'll find yourself doing U-turns during deployment. Probably many of them. As the suit-seller on television says, "I guarantee it."

Build up to the big picture, not down from it

From the standpoints of technology, data management and data integration, the toughest sales automation challenges are typically at or near the relationship management level. That's one reason you start there and design back toward your central information hub. The other reason, as we've discussed, is that relationship managers won't support a system that's not designed around their needs.

Critical Decisions

I'm not going to give you a checklist to slap on your clipboard and carry around as you implement sales automation…before lunch. Done this, done that, put the software on the loading dock. Right next to the laptops. Now, one from each pallet. Software, laptop, instruction manual, shackles, ball and chain…If you like working that way, there's a job at a quick lube place just awaiting for you. But then again, you wouldn't be reading this if you liked working that way. So I won't insult your intelligence with a checklist. Instead, I've tried to outline the common elements most of you will want to think hard about before you start your new data map.

NEAT, PREPACKAGED CHECKLISTS ARE FOR OIL CHANGES, NOT SALES AUTOMATION.

How many items of data will you track, and how specific are they to your business or industry?

Roughly how many individual items of information (fields) will you need in your database? Are they generic, or will you need to significantly customize any software system you use to have proper field names? How many folders (tables) will be needed to organize your data into logical groups? Keep in mind that sales automation is an exercise in discipline. Don't shoot for the moon and design a database incorporating everything you could ever want to know. You'll wind up knowing nothing, because relationship managers won't collect all that data for you and probably won't use the system.

What are you database structure requirements?

What data elements need to relate to each other? A practical way to arrive at an answer is to list out all the important fields of data, then imagine what reports you might want about each field and how many other fields you'll need to associate with each field. The lines between each principal data field and all the others you want to relate to it are your "data relationships," which determine how your database designer will make all of the intricate links between tables holding the data. Unless, that is, you bought a shrink-wrapped program with a flat file (non-relational database) that doesn't allow you to create many links among data beyond those preprogrammed for you.

How much data capacity is required?

That's a function of which data are important to you as well as how many customers and potential customers your reps have in their territories. One of the first questions a software provider will ask you is, "How many records (names or organizations) will you be managing?" The next question may be, "How many fields for each record?" These are good and necessary questions.

Does your database need to be fully relational?

The answer is almost always "yes, yes, yes," if you're going to incorporate anything more than basic contact data. Don't fall for the "unlimited number of user-defined fields" line on the retail box. Providing lots of customizable fields is a no-brainer. But you can't do much with the data these thousands of fields hold if they're in a flat file instead of a relational database. Most shrink-wrapped sales automation software packages lack fully relational databases. In fact, the part that's "relational" is typically tiny compared to the potential whole.

Does your system require open architecture?

Again, the answer is almost always "yes, yes, yes." It doesn't matter if you decide to limit your system to sales only, although you'll regret that later. In tomorrow's world (I mean almost literally, tomorrow) nothing will stay isolated from the customer information flow—except you, if you design a sales automation system that can't communicate with the rest of your world.

What about office automation links?

Among the principal missed opportunities is forgetting the importance of integrating sales automation with your office suite. Sales automation developers have been forgetting this for years, but now Microsoft has opened the door for such integration through the very open and friendly architecture of Outlook 97 and the rest of Office 97. As I write this book, IPC/Pipestream is beta testing a new RM program, Sales Continuum 98, which uses the Outlook 97 calendar and synchronizes with Outlook in one click of the mouse.

Of all the inducements to select Microsoft Office over another office suite, achieving office automation along with sales automation ranks at the top. Clientele appears headed that way, with its new sales automation module, and many more will certainly elect to establish links between their sales automation and the Office 97 environment. Fewer and fewer sales automation providers are bothering to build links to anything else.

What noncustomer data will be part of your sales automation system?

Noncustomer data such as sales presentations, product bulletins, complex equipment "fit-up" charts (which accessories can go with what equipment) can really add to your hardware requirements. And if you want relationship managers to have easy access to noncustomer data, you'll make that a software consideration as well.

What are your integration needs?

Cross-platform data integration (melding data across different operating systems such as Windows 95 and UNIX), as well as data integration between different software programs such as Windows 95 sales automation and project management software programs, will become much easier over time as software development continues to catch up with customer need for systems and data integration. But for now, you have to ask

A VALUABLE CORPORATE TOOL, LOTUS NOTES IS OFTEN SUBSTITUTED FOR SALES AUTOMATION — BUT IT DOESN'T DO THE SAME JOB.

the right questions to make sure you'll be able to accomplish desirable integration down the road, if not now. And don't let anyone jive you with "Java is coming." As an operating system, Java is a nonplayer in sales automation and, in my opinion, that's unlikely to change anytime soon. It's too anemic. Better-suited to pasty-faced "Webbies" who never see the light of day.

Besides, most of this Java-related, "thin platform" stuff you read about is really the last gap of hardware and software companies that "don't do desktop"—and IT professionals who don't want desktop. Too bad for them. Too late too. Desktop computer users, including sales automation users, have already experienced the power of full-powered desktop applications. None of that "Java-jive" for them. Java has very powerfull potential uses—but full desktop applications, especially sales automation, ain't among them.

How should we roll up individual databases?

That's a fancy way of saying, "How should we synchronize?" I used the fancy way because some nerd like me will spring that on you without warning. If you know what they're talking about, they'll know that you're a nerd, too.

Of primary concern is whether to use LAN-sync or WAN-sync. Other questions to answer now are, How much data should you synchronize? And are you going to have conflicts or compliance issues over synchronization with company relationship managers, independent reps or distributor reps, as the case may be?

Who's on which system?

Just as new technologies are on the way to rescue us from integration dilemmas, so too are new and improved attitudes about focusing our systems on customers instead of on internal needs. But until these attitudes arrive, you may have to struggle through cultural resistance, even to such questions as, "Why should customer service data stay on the 'main' system, rather than the sales automation system?" If you're really brave (or have a death wish), you might also entertain asking, "Shouldn't accounting draw their customer records from sales automation, rather than maintain parallel customer name and address records?" On the other hand, you may decide not to ask anything of the kind, even though in many organizations you could make a very strong case that there should be one, and only one, core customer record for each customer.

Recently, a client organization CEO gave me a single mandate regarding the design of a sales automation system. That was, "When you finish, I want one customer record that everyone uses. One." He has both foresight and courage. He's also in a high-tech industry and can visualize the possibilities for making that a reality. Before long, more will have his vision.

Systems and technical support.

In an ideal world, external technical limitations would not limit your sales automation horizons. In the real world, they do. One important question to ask is, "Can your organization support field office LANs?" Many extremely network-wise Fortune companies are only that wise at HQ. I recently worked with a client in the process of installing a SAP® operations system, the very pinnacle of technical sophistication. The field systems were in shambles. All of the good stuff was at corporate in operations. Everyone else had to fend for themselves.

Does your network server have adequate capacity?

Upgrading or replacing servers involves more than plopping down a new PC on a desk or tossing a sales rep a new laptop. And shifting multiple users off dumb terminals onto client-server networked PCs can be an IT adventure. Anticipate. Anticipate. Anticipate. By the way, if IT says that sales automation is going on an existing server that's running existing applications, do a little test. Ask users if batch-processing or just ordinary traffic during the workday ever slows down the network. If it does, sales automation needs an independent server. Period.

Is your installed base of laptops and PCs up to sales automation requirements?

In today's environment, 16 MB of RAM, Pentium processors, modems and 1 gigabyte or higher hard drive capacity are minimum laptop requirements. Some high-end sales automation software needs P166 or higher processing speed and even 32 MB RAM.

What database languages do you speak?

Software code, like the written word, comes in many different languages. Some, like PASCAL, are ancient and rarely spoken any more. Others, like FoxPro, have relatively few users. What does this matter, as long as some multilingual geek somewhere is going to put your databases together?

It may not. But if you're going to be building and linking auxiliary programs to create quotations or track up-to-the-minute product inventory, your sales automation database needs to be written in a language spoken by someone in your organization or in the local consulting community. In the barren landscape of North Dakota, you're unlikely to find someone who programs in B'trieve or Delphi or FoxPro. Visual Basic is the most common of the sales automation database languages, and the easiest to find programmers for, followed by SQL (both the query and database languages). Power Builder is gaining users, but still much harder to support.

It's a good idea to assess language skills before you start. The IT folks will ask who wound up your propeller, but getting caught without programming resources isn't funny.

Are you on Windows 95 yet?

You probably don't want to be retrofitting new hardware with dated software, and some newer sales automation packages run only on 32-bit Windows 95 operating systems.

Macs? Kiss 'em good-by.

OS/2? Forget it.

How much software customization are you planning?

You can bend software until it breaks. If you have to customize software too far, better look for a better system. And be careful not to create annuities for consultants (myself included) who help reconfigure your software. Let a software developer follow Bill Gates' zigs and zags, rather than having a heart attack yourself (not to mention a financial hemorrhage) every time Gates burps out a new operating system.

Do it in-house?

Never, never, never. "Homebrew" is poison. Don't touch it unless you like waiting three years for five-year-old technology that costs seven times as much and does just half of what a modified commercial package can do.

These are the most common issues. At least I hope I've hit them all. As you might notice, if you glance back at these questions, what I'm really doing is setting boundaries. Where your sales automation system has to go. Where it can't go. And what's realistic.

On the way to sales automation, you'll have to move some "soft walls" and boundaries, such as departmental territory lines and "no data traffic" signs. But you have to be very sanguine about what you can accomplish, especially in a short period of time. Of course, the good news here is that nothing systems-wise lasts very long anymore; so if something needs changing to accommodate sales automation, it may very well need changing for other reasons as well.

The Big Picture

Now you're ready to draw the "big picture"— your conceptual design. You should be able to express your sales automation system concept in several paragraphs of concise narrative. You, with the help of your new bosom buddy in IT, should include what operating systems you're going to use where; which data you're going to collect and manage; which application systems will be involved (other than sales automation); which cross-system links you'd like to have; whether you're going to build or buy sales automation software (always buy, but it helps to keep confirming that in writing); what types of hardware such as desktops, laptops or network servers you may need; a picture of the data flow among system levels; and the manner of synchronization.

A few paragraphs. And a lot of brain-numbing thinking and consideration leading up to them. Now you've finally reached the point where most organizations start, yes start, sales automation projects. But planning pays off, and those who take shortcuts pay dearly.

By the way, if you're still not ready to make some of the preliminary decisions described above, don't worry. Leave them until after you create your new data map. But it's helpful to take a stab at it, because knowing where you have to go and where you can't go is sort of fundamental when you're drawing up a new map. Any kind of map.

Here's a sample conceptual design.

SAMPLE CONCEPTUAL DESIGN

Our sales automation system will tie together field sales, sales management, customer service and marketing. In addition, information links will be created with accounting, technical service, logistics and inventory control. The two most important aspects of the system are managing sales as a *process* (we intend to incorporate sales activity cycles and cycle measurement into the database) and the communication between sales and customer service.

A single customer database will service sales, sales management and customer service. Each of these functions will have its own set of database controls, however. Because of the nature of our customers, the database will be built around organizations with multiple contacts, rather than individual contacts linked by organization. The database will proactively suggest sales cycle steps, triggered by projected capital equipment replacement schedules. The automation system will also provide pipeline management information for projecting both dollar sales and whole-goods unit inventory requirements.

Marketing will draw data from the sales automation system for the (direct) marketing database and feed qualified prospect information as well as all customer contacts to the automation system. A robust data link between the sales automation system and accounting will be required for transferring service and billing information. Bids and quotations will be converted into sales orders within the automation system, which will also generate invoices and post them to accounting. We will also require a real-time link with logistics so that sales and service can immediately identify order status. The technical service link does not have to be real time, and will only involve moving service statistics and summarized customer issues into their environment.

The sales automation database must be fully relational and capable of managing 100M customer and prospect records approximately 150 fields in length. The automation package must provide easy access and customer record linkage to Microsoft Office (not just Word). Document file libraries will be part of each customer record. We will synchronize field databases at the regional level, with more limited synchronization between regional offices and corporate. We are unsure at this point whether we will synchronize over the Web, or by using our Microsoft Exchange Server. The same question remains for product and pricing information and interactive product demonstration materials.

All network requirements appear to be met by our current in-place systems. However, we will need to upgrade all desktop units involved to Windows 95, and approximately half of our 300 in-service laptops will need significant upgrading or replacement. Any new laptops purchased should meet a *minimum* spec of P166 MHz processors with 16MB RAM, 1 gigabyte hard drives, active matrix screens, full-motion video, stereo sound with option for external speakers, 33.6K modems (internal preferred), and 16X CD-ROMs. Current company specs for desktops will suffice.

Aside from helping you stay on track while you draw up a new data map, this conceptual plan is a good way to update everyone who should know what you're up to. It's even a good "in-process sign-off" tool. A little communication goes a long way.

New Data Map

It's "deja vu all over again." Hope you saved your invitation list, because you'll need to replay your previous data mapping session. Only this time, you're building up instead of breaking down. This side of data mapping can be much more fun, but it has a downside as well. If it hasn't hit already, all of the potential internal dissonance I've mentioned tends to land squarely on the conference room table at this point. Once you finalize a new data map, the die is cast in terms of sales automation design. Past this point, your project should crest the mountain you've been climbing and start building up steam. Although a sales automation project can still get derailed past this point (and many have), unless you've left someone important out of the process, the "derailer" may might have to throw his or her body across the tracks to overcome your momentum.

This is a good time to pretend you and your project are "the little engine that could." If you have young children, you might even read the book as the bedtime story. You'll amuse them and encourage yourself.

Start mapping at the point of customer contact

Among the more frequent mistakes made when designing sales automation systems is designing from a central data collection point, located at corporate, outward to the point of customer contact. This happens frequently when organizations try to force-fit sales automation around a (direct) marketing data warehouse. It also happens when corporate executives have a strong "corporate first" mindset.

But no matter how many times it happens, it never works. I'll say it again, for emphasis.

Designing sales automation outward from corporate never works.

Unfortunately, that doesn't seem to deter organizations with a "corporate first" culture.

Remember, sales automation is a relationship management tool first, and a corporate tool second. Don't fall for traps such as, "We're not doing sales automation, just figuring out a way to ship data to the field." If you expect the field to use the data you send to relationship managers, you're doing sales automation. And that means you're subject to the laws of nature—and relationship management behavior—that govern sales automation deployment.

Relationship management needs come first

That's true in terms of what data goes into the system, what data comes out of the system at the relationship management level and how data is shared. That's why you start mapping at the contact level.

Although, I must hasten to identify two common, sales-perceived needs that don't come first. In fact, they get left behind during sales automation deployment.

Sales "ownership" of customer data

Among salespeople, there's a traditional perspective that relationship managers "own" their customer data. They can't, not in an information age. Not without severely handicapping their organization. The day is soon coming when even independent distributors and dealers will routinely come under pressure to share customer data with suppliers and manufacturers in exchange for greater marketing and sales support. It's already happening in some distribution systems, although only with mixed results because most organizations remain better at taking than giving. Fortunately, attempts to get closer to customers are forcing more and more organizations out of that mold.

Don't let considerations like "they'll never give up that data" influence your data mapping. If they're your salespeople, you own the data. Period.

Resistance to activity measurement

No one likes people looking over their shoulder. Not me, not you, not anyone. None of us works efficiently 100% of the time. Heck, none of us "works" 100% of our time. Yours truly used to have a couple of mythical business associates (or customers, when I was selling) called "Mr. Bass" and "Mr. Pike." I went a whole summer in Minneapolis having frequent sunny afternoon meetings with one or the other, and "smoked" a secretary from the great outdoors of Northern Minnesota the whole time. Until one Friday in September, when she asked me, "Who is Mr. Pike?" I guess I pushed it a little far when I answered, "Oh, you mean Wally Pike?" Almost a scene straight out of *Fargo*. But I could still run then, too.

Your first instinct might be to say, "Hey, those lazy sales reps deserve some real scrutiny." I hope not. Not because some sales reps couldn't clean up their act a little, or even a lot, but because sales managers often are more resentful of the intrusion caused by activity measurement than are their reps. Did you ever hear a sales manager say, "You can ask me how we're doing. But don't ask me how we're getting it done." Lots of variations on that theme out there. Sorry, but "how you're getting it done" has everything to do with outcomes. Sales is a process, and the "how" matters very much.

If you run into that noise from sales managers, remind them that there's no way to identify and adopt best practices without measuring sales activities.

Don't let anticipated resistance alter your data mapping, either. We live in a measurable world. There's no place to hide from that anymore. Well, maybe hide a little.

Map by data type

Mapping data by type, such as core customer information or transaction history, all the way from data origination right through to discarding dead or dying data, works much better than mapping at one time all data that moves through one specific work station. In most circumstances, the best place to start is with a customer's name and address. You'd be surprised at how many times a single customer's name and address can be hand-keyed into one organization's information systems, then separately maintained on different systems that don't communicate. I recently worked with a client organization where, to book a new customer, the customer name had to be entered 13 times.

Matter of fact, it still does. Part way through the planning process the client acquired a competitor that was trying to use a shelf-unstable ICM as the basis for sales automation. Unfortunately, expanding that system was a cheap and easy way for management to put a check mark beside sales automation. Or change it from red to black, the way the detectives on television's "Homicide" do when they solve a case. Ugly outcome. Very ugly. Murdered the data. Killed it dead. But they didn't do in my very savvy customer contact. I helped her find a better job with a new client with more smarts.

Not to digress too far, health care organizations are among those most often afflicted by "multiple customer record disease." Based on my incoming mail, software companies do a pretty good job of it, too.

Clean up all the messes you can

As you map, be particularly aware of parallel data movements, duplicate data, repetitive data entry and especially those nasty black holes where valuable customer data dead-end and die. Your new data map should all but eliminate these messes. Your initial implementation will fall short of cleaning up all of them, but at least know how you plan to finish the job over time.

Connect all the dots

When you finish, every piece of customer information should have a point of origin, a predetermined route to travel and a planned exit from the system at a certain age or upon subsequent override. Similarly, the flow of product and other information valuable to relationship managers, and customers too, must be mapped out in detail, including all necessary data updating and verification procedures.

The charts on the next two pages show how the previous examples of initial data mapping change when we redesign the data flow, this time starting at the point of customer contact.

Compare the new maps with the originals. The new set is so much cleaner and simpler. That always happens.

Information systems designed from the point of customer contact in toward operations are almost invariably much simpler and more streamlined than systems designed to meet internal needs first. Wonder why?

ROUGH CUT VIEW REVISED

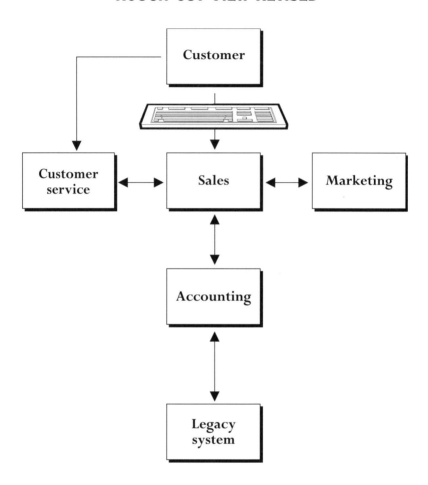

The re-mapped customer data flow is much simpler and involves only one key entry of basic customer information. It's also paperless.

Detail: Data Flow Through Sales

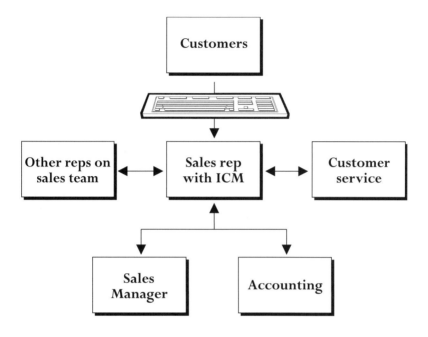

The detail chart is simplified even more after re-mapping data.

FUNCTIONAL DESIGN

By now, any software vendors you've been talking to are chomping at the bit. From their perspective, you're being a bad customer. You're not buying, so you must be procrastinating. Your management, perhaps even your sponsors, are probably getting impatient as well. But stay the course. In sales automation, as in most aspects of life, the devil is in the details. Work them out first. Everyone (except the software vendors eager for your order) will appreciate you for doing it right.

Sales automation database design

Once again, start this process at the primary point of customer contact. Although database marketing types will argue this, the primary point of customer contact must be the pivot point of your whole system. Think hard, however, about which point of customer contact to designate as "primary." In most organizations, it's sales. But in a significant number, customer service sits at the synapse of sales and business operations, and anchoring sales automation system in service makes sense. Coincidentally, whichever relationship management function turns out to be your best starting point will usually be the one that presents the greatest challenges in database design. More lines coming in. More going out.

By comparison with sales automation, (direct) marketing databases or data warehouses are easier to construct. More complex in a narrow technical sense, but much less critical. Data warehouses don't deal with work process or human behavior (except for making some of us yawn).

In any process, sales automation development included, you're best off solving the difficult problems first. Leave the grinding and milling of data in "da warehouse" for later.

Although relationship managers aren't database designers, at this point in the deployment process you should be joined at the hip with several experienced relationship managers of each type present in your organization—sales reps, customer service reps, telemarketers (hopefully not the one you swore at last night during dinner). Sales managers and marketing managers are also important to the process, but remember, *sales and marketing management interests rarely coincide with relationship management interests.* Here, as in other steps in the functional design process, "Wear your dancin' shoes."

Also, if you need to get outside help designing your sales automation database, get someone experienced in *sales automation database design,* not (direct) marketing database stuff. The two are worlds apart, as I learned the first time I crossed over the line from (direct) marketing to sales automation. First time out

IMPLEMENTING SALES AUTOMATION REQUIRES A HEAP OF DIPLOMACY.

I focused too much on marketing communication and too little on sales process. Fortunately, just when we were ready to roll, my client called off the whole marketing initiative the system was designed to support. Lucky me. My mistakes never saw the light of day. And I didn't make them again.

But let's presume you're going to handle it internally. Just how do you develop a *functional design* for your sales automation system?

It's much easier than you might think. And it's also a way for you to get very close to the nitty-gritty of what's about to happen without being a propeller-head.

Here's how you do it. Four easy steps.

1. Work with your sales and service colleagues (and their managers) to *identify the sequence of data* use for each. On the following page, you'll see an example of a customer service sequence for a high-tech firm with field technicians. Sales is less linear than service,

but you can define a series of sequences for each major sales activity—making sales calls, initiating proposals, product demonstrations, forecasting, scheduling future actions...Everything they need or want to do.

2. Describe *all the reports you want* from the system. It's amazing how much information about final database format and structure can be gleaned from the reports desired. (An absolute wizard in customer research by the name of David Mangen, president of Mangen Research Associates in Minneapolis, taught me this trick while we were working together on a customer research project.)

3. Grab *your new data maps and your conceptual design.* You just finished these, so you should be able to find them.

4. *Throw a binder clip around the items listed in steps 1-3.* You may want to add a cover memo and format them uniformly, even add a few transition paragraphs, but that's all you need.

DATA USE SEQUENCE - CUSTOMER SERVICE

1. Receive call at Help Desk from service customer.
2. Capture caller name.
3. Pull up customer record (by company name).
4. Query customer for correct site (if multiple) and select.
5. Get verbatim description of problem.
6. Identify problem equipment (best by ID#).

7. Check service contract coverage for that ID#; inform caller of how much left on contract.

8. Confirm billing rate with customer.

9. Determine response time (dictated by contract type).

10. Check for "credit alert" (data batch imported from Great Plains Dynamics).

11. Review service history for that ID# (if appropriate).

12. Review service history for that customer (if appropriate).

13. Enter hot-key to assign MAR#.

14. Assign a problem code.

15. Assign service priority.

16. Identify call-back name and number.

17. Assign a service code (which identifies which tech, qualifications needed).

18. Identify service contract/warranty coverage (if any) on equipment, software, OS, network.

19. Check "primary's" availability.

20. Call up list of other techs with appropriate service code rating.

21. View their schedules (need group calendar) and their location on Twin Cities metro map (optional).

22. Select tech for assignment.

23. Complete call.

24. Schedule tech on master tech calendar.

25. E-mail partial customer record to tech's mailbox.

26. Beep tech to alert that next service call in mailbox.

27. Set alarm to escalate if message not picked up by set time (on-screen escalation message).

28. Tech receives record from e-mail.

29. Calls customer contact with e.t.a.

30. Calls (or e-mails) Help Desk to confirm contact, schedule.

31. If schedule problem, Help Desk calls up "qualified" list of backup techs (repeat 23-29).

32. Tech reviews record before meeting contact, enters start time.

33. When job complete, tech enters time, notes about service, parts used, units swapped.

34. Tech assigns RMA (Help Desk can also assign in obvious situations).

35. Tech records parts used from "trunk inventory."

36. Tech e-mails to Help Desk for re-integration of record into customer database.

Now we're ready for the next implementation phase. The one where WE FINALLY GET TO PICK THE DAMNED SOFTWARE. But that's the second step in Phase III.

PHASE III

SALES AUTOMATION DEPLOYMENT MAP

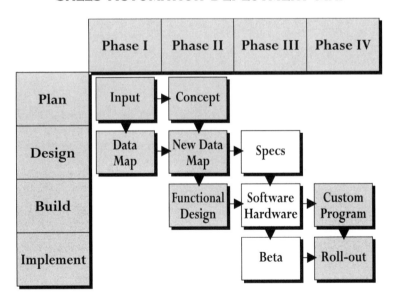

	Phase I	Phase II	Phase III	Phase IV
Plan	Input	Concept		
Design	Data Map	New Data Map	Specs	
Build		Functional Design	Software Hardware	Custom Program
Implement			Beta	Roll-out

Selecting software comes toward the end of the deployment process, not at the beginning.

If you thought you were running fast before, wait until you get closer to that fateful moment...picking software. Actually, it's usually a bust as big moments go. You've done so much prep that your decision is almost made for you. Boy, planning spoils all the fun, doesn't it.

Actually, your biggest concern at this juncture may be all the people breathing down your neck, wanting the system done and in their hands RIGHT NOW. Hold your ground and tell them to go do some stuff. You might also want to ask your guardian angel sponsor to spray you with sales and marketing repellent to keep the pests away. Service already has a system, so they're a lot more patient.

TECHNICAL SPECIFICATIONS

Oh no, not more of this. Anything but this.

Relax. I'm going to give you a quick and painless way to do a long and tedious job. But it's a job you don't ever want to skip, because lack of detailed specifications could rise up and bite you hard. That's especially true if you find yourself in a dispute with an outside vendor, like a software developer.

Here's how you do specs while you sit at the local coffee salon crying in your mocha mud frappe over having this assignment in the first place.

You cheat.

In fact, I'll give you three easy, deliciously deceitful ways to get specs done without doing them yourself.

1. *Hire a consultant* experienced in sales automation system design. Just make sure they do sales automation, not that other stuff.

2. *Beg IT to do it.* But offer to take them golfing and fishing and "tennising" when you do.

3. *Team up IT with the software supplier* you're about to select and have them do it together.

If IT can't do it or you can't find an experienced outside resource—in other words, you're desperate—you can fall back on your functional design for making a preliminary software decision. Many software suppliers encourage that, preferring to write their own set of specifications specifically for their system. But don't let them cheat by altering your design to fit their system's capabilities. You must be very vigilant about this if the software supplier, not you, writes any or all of the technical specifications for your sales automation system. Best advice—offer to pay the software developer you believe you'll select to write the specs. Then sign on the dotted line for the overall purchase only after you've approved their specifications.

Finish your mocha. And smile. You're heading down the home stretch.

Software Selection

Okay, no more heavy breathing. The magic moment has arrived. You're ready to select sales automation software. A few die-hard, "speed-is-life" readers might say, "Gee, we're finally ready to start sales automation." Wise guys. But these jokers are about to realize how far off base they are—because there's not much left to select from, in terms of sales automation software.

Without knowing it, you've probably eliminated all but several software packages from consideration. Sure, some 500 or more sales automation software packages may be vying for your attention. But sales automation is a very young industry, not nearly mature enough to include large numbers of parity products. So you probably won't find too many of those 500 or more packages right for your application. Plus, discarding the unfortunately high percentage of products that are either mediocre performers or overpriced, or both, will narrow your field even further. If you have four or five strong software options after you've completed your specifications (or functional design), that's a lot. In contrast, the "speed-is-lifers" are still wading through the whole stack—and they're still likely to pass over the best choices.

Think of sales automation as a marathon. Those who start out sprinting, because they only know how to go fast, make it part way through and then die at the sidelines, sucking air and water as you stride by them. Patience pays, at least it does in sales automation.

So, how do you actually identify those four or five or two or seven software programs that best meet your needs?

Here are the principal criteria I use.

Process fit

If you don't thoroughly understand your work processes—and not just superficially—you can't select the right software. You have to guess. But if you've done your data mapping and matched information flow to work flow, you can zero in on a relatively small number of sales automation software programs that will effectively support your processes.

As you might expect, the higher in price range you go, the higher the percentage of programs there is that pass the "process fit" profile. But your object shouldn't be throwing money at the job, spending enough to make sure you can do whatever it turns out you need to do, whenever you happen to find that out. Instead, you should start with establishing your needs, then identify how much you need to spend in order to meet those needs. Not that I'm in any way advocating least-cost solutions. But realistically, sales automation is virtually always under-funded. Blow everything you have on software, leaving nothing for testing and training and rollout support, and you'll waste your whole investment in that star-spangled sales automation software that makes toast and coffee in the morning.

Here's a tip. You can "top line" process fit by checking for compatibility with your most critical processes first. Chances are, whichever programs meet your fundamental needs will follow through and meet the great majority of whatever else you need to accomplish. Or you can modify the program to meet remaining unmet needs. That's because most sales automation packages reflect the developer's perspective on how sales and marketing activities unfold. If the top-line vision matches yours or your organization's, chances are that most of the details will as well.

Of course, most shrink-wrapped, ICM and GCM software developers carefully avoid expressing a perspective, preferring to be generic instead. They can sell more copies that way. To customers who don't know any better. But not you. Sales automation is one market where you should always avoid companies attempting to achieve market share leadership. In sales automation, achieving market share is synonymous with providing generic solutions.

That reminds me of a conversation I had recently with a maker of "linking software" that ties sales automation software to a popular corporate accounting system. This very small company claims to hold the key to unlocking the full potential of sales automation software and making it an enterprise solution. Funny though. The only sales automation packages it provides links for are the most generic, and thereby the programs with the least potential to ever become enterprise-anything. When I questioned the company "guru" about this strange combination of enterprise links to nonenterprise sales automation software, he condescendingly responded, "We're after market share. We're not going to fool around with anything that doesn't have high-volume potential."

Would somebody please put the rubber band back on his propeller? And teach him the difference between "product" and "solution?"

Resources

Finding the end of the ball of string on a software search can be frustrating if you don't live in the sales automation industry, so here's a tip. A gentleman named Rich Bohn, of the Denali Group in Washington, runs a software research service. Good guy. He makes sure you've done your planning first. Better guy. You can call him at 206-392-3514 or hit the Web site at www.sellmorenow.com. Bohn writes reviews for a new monthly magazine called Sales and Field Force Automation. Sales process consultant Barry Trailer, mentioned earlier, writes for SFFA, too. If your sales lack process call him at 408-293-8664. SFFA Subscription info is available at 800-332-5264 or www.so@hutchins.com. It's a good read. Check it out.

Features

Functionality does not mean fancy screens, colorful icons and a gazillion bells and whistles. Yes, a well-designed, graphical user

interface (GUI) will encourage use. But an interface so splat-
tered with icons that your computer looks like a pigeon
squatted over the screen is more off-putting than DOS. The best
way to evaluate program features, including the GUI, is to try
it. Let a few particularly cooperative relationship managers give
it a whirl and run it through its paces, preferably with live data.
Also use it yourself to manage your calendar and office automation functions. Even if you have to buy several test copies of a
software package or two, do it.

And while you're doing test drives, don't let anyone hurry
you—anyone inside or outside. And what's the potential software vendor doing while you test? If the commission year is
ending, you may need more sales rep repellent about now.

Reliability

Sad to say, many sales automation software programs on the
market, including several "best sellers," are poorly engineered
or poorly supported or both. Pay no attention to claims of "#1"
or a long list of logos from trade magazines recommending a
particular program. You're very unlikely to find the right program on a retail shelf, which makes it unlikely that your best solution will bother to claim to be #1. And PC-related magazine reviews are only helpful if you want a system for yourself and no one else. These critiques rarely go more than skin deep into integration, open architecture and other issues that concern organizational rather than personal buyers.

TEST-DRIVE SALES AUTOMATION SOFTWARE BEFORE YOU COMMIT.

Fortunately, the Relationship Manager (RM) category of
sales automation software is growing by leaps and bounds, and
prices are coming down as well. You now have a clear, and in

most cases preferable, alternative to either brutally high-ticket stuff, "home brew," or shrink-wrapped nonsolutions.

Regardless of which sales automation category you intend to use, don't take vendor claims on faith. Talk to other users and get the true facts before you buy. Make sure you talk to network users and users who rely on remote synchronization (if you will be synchronizing). Networking and synchronization are two of the more problematic areas.

Scalability

Sales automation scalability is coming, but coming slowly. Before long, software companies won't get away with asking you to blow $1,500 or $2,000 on high-powered software for each and every sales and service rep in your organization. After all, you're paying all that money to get enterprise sales automation. By definition, *enterprise sales automation* has different functions for different user groups, many of which have no reason to be on a sale rep's laptop. Those believing they can continue the practice of charging total license fees for every user are smoking rope.

Bottom line, there's no need to squeeze a full-priced, every-feature version of an expensive software program onto the highest capacity laptop you can find—except that the software company hasn't yet developed a scalable product. Atlanta-based Optima Technologies solves this problem by building Teamworks out of individual applets for each major function and charging each user for only the applets they need. Others should follow its example.

In the interim, while smart software developers are designing scalable programs, try negotiating scalable pricing. Remember, software sellers' per-license costs are virtually nil. They have plenty of negotiating room to set prices consistent with the functionality you can actually use at the relationship management level.

Customization

There are three sides to this issue: two extremes and a new opportunity. You probably want to be somewhere between the two extremes, somewhere close to the middle. I'll talk about the "new opportunity" in a minute.

One extreme is the "use it out of the box" approach, which indicates that not much thought is going into this sales automation project. Better software suppliers don't offer the option of loading three disks or a CD, selecting 10 variable fields and calling it quits. Packages like that "fake" it. True sales automation software is a set of specialized controls sitting over a fully relational database. Adapting both the controls and the database to the unique needs of each organization is what makes sales automation so powerful. You should anticipate considerable customization of your sales automation software. A lot more than you can customize retail software. And don't let those computer magazine reviews fool you. When they talk about all the custom data fields you can create, that's literally what they're talking about—custom fields. Can't do much with them when the database isn't fully relational. But they're there. For looks. And they do fool the reviewers.

DON'T GET CARRIED AWAY WITH SOFTWARE CUSTOMIZATION.

The other extreme is overcustomization. A good example is a project I worked on just prior to introduction of the last wave of new and improved software. We were developing a sales automation program for one division of a multidivisional manufacturing organization. For a variety of unfortunate reasons, and despite our numerous attempts, we were unable to engage other divisions up-front. That scared us, because there wasn't an affordable (in our client's terms) software program available with enough horsepower to accomplish much more than our initial assigned task. But onward with development we went, until after beta testing, when the potential of sales automation leaked to other business units; at which point, we were confronted with a blizzard of new needs and requests.

Unfortunately, we had already stretched the original software program to the limit. In fact, we had modified the base program until it was almost unrecognizable. This situation was further aggravated by the customer-unfriendly software developer that steadfastly refused to allow us to combine all the add-ons required to meet the original needs on one CD with their program, which made loading it a nightmare. We couldn't stretch it any further without risking a fate far worse than switching to new software.

Fortunately for us, during the development cycle WinSales had introduced a major upgrade, WinSales 3.0 (the predecessor to Client Vision), which offered extensive customization of a truly relational database plus powerful process management features—at a GCM price. Without it, we would have been up the network without a paddle. Still, the switch cost the client considerable dollars and delay.

But all sales automation software, even the most customizable, has its breaking point. While most GCMs crumble like pretzels under a boot heel if you subject them to much stress, you can torque the better RMs a bunch. But not to the ends of the earth. If you find yourself straining at the limits of your software, or with more customization than designed-in capabilities, you're almost certainly on the wrong program. Cut your losses and switch. Better to switch to a better program while you're still in development than put out a balky, unreliable product that no one will use.

Back in the beginning of this discussion on customization, I mentioned a "new opportunity." Frankly, I wouldn't recommend this opportunity to everybody. Not even to most clients. But for some—especially those with a strong, development-oriented IT unit—the opportunity is now emerging to buy sales automation controls and build your own custom database beneath them, using commercial database engines such as Access, Sequel Server, Oracle, Sybase and Informix. However, going beyond Sequel Server into the latter, more powerful environments can put you into a world of hurt from the both a financial and a practical standpoint. If you need more sophistication (or capacity) for sales automation software than Sequel Server-based programs provide, chances are that some data warehouse proponents arrived in a Trojan horse and infiltrated your project. Catch them and burn them at the stake.

Remember, first and foremost, sales automation automates and supports *processes carried out by human beings*. And we humans are only so sophisticated and can only handle a modicum of complexity in our activities. For consistency's sake, you may opt to work in databases used elsewhere in the enterprise such as Oracle, Sybase or Informix. But doing so exposes you to the risk of overdoing it and getting too fancy for the human participants.

All that said, if you have to choose between IT developing the database under purchased sales automation controls or having IT build the controls, too, definitely choose the former. In fact, throw your body across the tracks to keep the latter from happening. Because it will never happen. At least not in a time frame or budget you can afford.

Size

It goes without saying that your sales automation software must have the capacity to hold all the data you need to manage, both in terms of the number of relational data fields and tables, and also in terms of sheer number of records. So why do so many sales automation implementers wind up in systems that come up short—in either record size, number of records or both? Because so many scale the size of their projects down to the size they want them to be, or to the size their budgets permit, rather than the size they need to be.

As the mechanic on the oil filter commercial used to say, "You can pay me now, or pay me later" (and I don't mean me, personally). The only thing you gain by going too small with your software program's data management capacity is the opportunity to have this much fun a second time.

One more note about size. Don't ever combine two limited-capacity databases to make one larger one. You may think you can "cheat" by using an add-on VAR software program or unre-

BEWARE OF ADDING VAR PROGRAMS TO OVERCOME BASE-PACKAGE-SOFTWARE SHORTCOMINGS, ESPECIALLY DATABASE SHORTCOMINGS.

lated software to extend your sales automation software's core database capabilities. If you do it and get away with it, would you please write me? You'll be the first I know of.

Please keep in mind, however, that scabbing two databases into one has no relation to the very workable practice of making software controls that fit over a variety of databases. Add-on utilities like quote programs and product demonstrations are also fine. But trying to create a core database out of two separate programs, even if the database extender is "authorized," is too dicey for my tastes. I call these "articulated" databases—they try to help the bus go around corners that busses can't go around. Great in the city. But sales automation is an Alpine road without guardrails. You take the bus. I'll settle for the sports car.

Code

Breaking with past industry practices, two service automation software developers, IMC Tiger Paw and Applied Business Services, now offer to sell their program code.[14] Both are written in Visual Basic. Theoretically, that means you can modify these programs almost at will. Realistically, it means you can also screw them up royally, and screw yourself up as well.

For most sales automation users, buying source code is more of a threat than an opportunity. But a good sales automation program will come with "macro-level code" that enables you to create new data tables, change the screen appearance, build different screens for different user groups (such as sales and service) and the like. If you are considering a program that doesn't come with macro-level code sufficient to make these modifications, reject it. Outright.

Linkages

Check to see that the programs you're considering are OBDC compliant. Observing industry conventions for data transfer among disparate databases gives you some level of assurance that you'll be able to move data among databases as you need to, although not necessarily with the speed and elegance you'd like. Supporting protocols such as OLE (object linking and exchange) automation and DDE (dynamic data exchange) is also a big plus if you're heading for enterprise-level sales automation. You'll be able to readily update data across programs, as long as both programs support the protocol.

By the way, never, ever, ever select a sales automation program that uses a custom-designed database. Any sales

---

[14] Both companies also offer sales automation capabilities, with IMC Tiger Paw selling a separate sales automation program that shares a database with its service companion. However, in both cases the sales automation components fall far short of the service functionality.

automation developer believing they can out-design the dedi-cated database (as opposed to sales automation) developers is likely on a grand ego trip, and furthermore doesn't understand that sales automation is about controls more than database design. Fortunately, there are relatively few of these home-brew databases around. Even if a particular developer employs Einstein in its database department, the chances that you would be able to link up the resulting brilliant design with much of anything else are slim.

The software developer

Thought you were going to get off easy, didn't you? Just a pick a software package and go right to work.

It's not quite that easy. Sales automation is a new field that's virtually exploded in the past three years. Typical of any market like this, when lots of product (software) first hits the market, not all of the suppliers "stick." Even suppliers of good product go under, due to bad marketing, bad distribution and under-capitalization. And makers of inferior products that have effective marketing, strong distribution and big bucks behind them sometimes make it. Accordingly, you can not assume that,

good product = good company, nor that

good company = good product.

You gotta go find out. The chart on the next two pages gives you some good guidelines to follow in identifying whether a company is going to sink, even though its product can swim, or vice versa. It also provides tips for determining if a software company is interested in your business; because, if they're not, boy do you have problems.

If you're only buying ten software licenses, you may have difficulty getting some of these questions answered (unless you're going to buy a boatload of consulting time). But it never hurts to ask.

And by the way, "Have you ever done anything in our industry?" is an irrelevant question, except in very particular cases like high-tech customer service, which requires a very unique database structure. Except in a small percentage of cases, the processes you're automating are much more specific to the organizations than to their industries. Now, if you want to ask, "Have you ever automated a company with processes similar to ours?" that's a darned *relevant* question.

SIZING UP A SOFTWARE COMPANY

1. Company Size?

If the supplier has fewer than 10 employees, it probably lacks critical mass. But it may be worth a shot. If it has more employees than you do, forget it; you'll never get any attention.

2. How long in business?

Being a start-up shouldn't rule the supplier out, if it's new, be extra careful that the company is either profitable or very well financed.

3. How many installations?

Have you ever heard the expression, "Never buy dot oh," (the first version)? That's too strict, but if the supplier has less than 25 installations, it's still working bugs out of its system—almost guaranteed.

4. References?

Don't buy without them. And make sure you call references from similar-sized companies.

5. Size/experience of engineering staff?

Lots of automation software companies are founded by technically-oriented salespeople. Don't buy from anyone that doesn't have an in-house staff of "plastic pocket-liner" folks (and "staff" means more than one). The best of all circumstances is a supplier that does consulting as well as software. That's a reasonable assurance that every engineer in the joint won't be preoccupied preparing the next release when you experience a technical problem.

6. Nature of distribution?

If retail is the primary distribution mode (or even a major distribution mode), forget it. If it works out of the box, it's not likely to work for you unless you have a cut-and-dried business and fewer than 10 system users.

7. Average installation size?

If it typically does 10 license installations and you have 110, think twice. If the supplier averages 1,000 licenses per customer, and you have 10, you won't matter.

8. Will the supplier supply code?

Only in very rare instances will you ever see program code, but you *need* macro-level code for customizing unless you want to be held captive for the life of your installation.

9. Does it supply financials?

Probably not, unless it's a public company. But you deserve specific enough information to satisfy your accountants that it's a safe choice.

10. Merger/acquisition candidate?

If your supplier merges or gets acquired during installation, you could be a customer pressured to "go away." This is a hard answer to get, but some may tell the truth.

11. Will it allow "melded" installation?

Don't, don't, don't accept a product that won't let you merge installation files with those of companion programs you'll be installing. Unless, that is, your eager to send an engineer out every time you load a new remote computer.

12. Will you get personal attention?

Press for an answer, if you have to. And make sure the person giving you "personal attention" isn't the billing clerk.

13. Will you have an assigned contact?

You should have an advocate in case something goes wrong. The "advocate" may value his or her job more than you, but assume the best.

There's quite a shakeout coming in the sales automation software industry, so don't be shy about protecting your interests.

After you select

Hey, that was so easy that I'll bet you're ready to jump all over a few more little details. No? Sorry, but you have to.

Connections

After you select software, you have to plan out synchronization among peer software users; plan synchronization to/from each level of users; plan synchronization with the hub database, which may or may not be the sales automation program; and design inputs and outputs to other databases. Sounds like a lot to do. It is, so just take it a step at a time. And, of course, start at the primary point of customer contact and work back.

If your work so far has left your relationship with IT a little strained, now is a good time to buy those folks a regal lunch. Maybe an afternoon round of golf, tennis or fishing. You need a strong technology partner to design and built the system integration elements of sales automation, unless you're working with a very low volume of data from a single source. Even if you're relying on outside programming and integration resources, you must involve IT.

Hub database

If there's a marketing database or customer data warehouse built and waiting to swallow up your sales automation data, you'll soon discover that it's improperly configured, possibly beyond repair. It almost has to be that way. Someone designed it without knowing your applications first, and blind luck is about all that will save this situation. If you're staring into the cavernous jaws of a predesigned data warehouse that's hungry for your data, placate it (and the people who built it) by feeding it your data. But create your real hub database within the sales automation software environment. If necessary for high-speed processing of high volumes of data, offload sales automation data to a "pure"

BEWARE OF HUNGRY DINOSAURS ANXIOUS TO EAT YOUR CATCH OF DATA.

database program that's not saddled with all the sales automation-required data relationships that slow processing speed. That's a much better alternative than just loading all your information into a "data dump" to be eaten and then slowly regurgitated as meaningless reports and analyses. But the best alternative is to get a beefy enough sales automation software system to do it all.

Hardware

Finally, it's a good idea to recheck your hardware specifications after you select software, in case your chosen software requires more horsepower than you anticipated (guaranteed it's not going to require less). Be careful to write clear and accurate hardware specifications for each user level. And don't let obsolete hardware restrain your system design. The software you're building should outlast even new hardware, and there's no point in underdeveloping the sales automation system to accommodate 486 desktops or low RAM laptops.

Software bloat is an unfortunate reality that we all have to live with. Digitized product information is a more pleasant reality. But both require lots of hard drive space, RAM and processor speed. Don't skimp on your specs.

BETA TESTING

You might wonder why I placed beta testing here in the implementation sequence, rather than after software customization
and after everything is set and ready to go. Good question.
Actually, some software customization does have to take place
before you release your sales automation system to trial users,
but much of it should occur concurrently with beta testing and
even after the sales automation system rollout begins. Two reasons for this:

1. By now, *eager potential users are calling you every five
    minutes,* wondering where their system is. Replies
    such as, "We're taking the time to do it right," wear
    thin about now. Better to release a basic system with
    the right basic data fields, several reports and not
    much else, than risk your sanity any further (you've
    risked it a lot, already).

2. Even more importantly, *you'll overwhelm all but the
    most computer-savvy users if you release the entire system
    at once.* And that's no joke.

Learning technology is like climbing a steep hill for lots of
folks. Let them take things one step at a time. Among the worst
risks you can take is to risk user rejection at your test sites.

Safe and successful beta testing

Remember the old Chinese proverb:

No one tests the depth of the water with both feet.

Spoon-feed your system to users, even to the point of generating user pressure on you to go faster. The list on the
following page presents a good test sequence for a sales-cen-
tered system. Unfortunately, with customer service you almost

have to cut over all at once, but only following a dry-run test by several customer service reps.

Beta Test Program

Select at least two test sites.

Use locations with friendly local (or regional) sales managers who want sales automation badly. Also try to select sites with a "techie" present who can be your local systems administrator.

Huddle with the sales managers and best rep or two at each site.

The best reps are the least likely to start using a new sales automation system. They may not use it even if use is mandatory. Unless, that is, you get them on your side before you start. You can't afford to have them *not* use the system. The sales managers will know best how to work with these reps.

Provide Windows 95 training to all users (assuming you're running Windows 95).

Be realistic. You can't expect your test users to come to sales automation training prepared. If you don't provide *mandatory* Windows 95 training a week or so before unveiling your sales automation software, you'll regret it. If you can manage to get three consecutive training days (a rarity), you can use the first day for Windows training.

Hold sales automation software training.

Hold it off-site. Including as many inside support people and other non-sales users as possible (they're usually more computer literate and can help bring balky sales-people along). And *sell the entire rationale for what you're doing.* If sales understand the importance (and inevitability) of sales automation, along with "what's in it for them," compliance will come much more readily.

Introduce only the most basic sales automation functions.

Initially introduce only the basic customer record, calendar scheduling, sales activity tracking and reporting, and several elements that sales really wants—usually e-mail, a quote program and anything else simple that will reduce paperwork.

Transfer their customer information for them.

Arrange just before training to transfer all customer data over to the new system. If they're already using another software program, depopulate it (which is a good security point—do not allow customer data to be stored on unauthorized, personal databases or contact managers).

Offer incentives for system utilization.

Set up sales contests that reward reps for completing customer records with all data. Make sure the contests are in no way punitive, and offer equal opportunities to all reps.

Encourage feedback.

Test users are your eyes and ears. Get every scrap of feedback you can.

The "Training" section, in Phase IV of this book, provides additional information helpful to setting up and running your beta sites.

Evaluation

Evaluating beta site results is a tricky process. You're going to have some excellent input regarding changes you should make (unless you're so good and so lucky that everything is perfect). You'll get silence from some reps who shrug and say it's okay. You'll have to corner these individuals and drag feedback out of them. Then you'll have the complainers, who typically come from both ends of the spectrum, the best and the worst reps.

You have to hear these folks out, but keep in mind that you're not designing your sales automation system for them. You probably have reps that no sales automation will help because they're beyond help. You also may have reps who are so good at managing their sales process internally that no external system will dramatically improve their results. A sales automation system will shed light on why these top reps are so good and how their "best practices" can be incorporated into the activity management portion of the system. Tracking low-end rep performance isn't very useful. Those folks are typically blaming everybody else for their failure, and they're unlikely to enter accurate performance data.

THE BEST AND THE WORST OF YOUR SALES FORCE WON'T BENEFIT FROM SALES AUTOMATION— BUT THE MIDDLE TWO-THIRDS WILL.

Sift through the feedback. Use the good stuff. Ignore the complaints from the "beyond help" group. If you can't respond to well-meaning suggestions, take the time to explain to those who made the suggestions just why you can't. Maybe it's due to system limitations or because the request stems from a personal idiosyncrasy. Not that any of us ever suffer from those things.

The relationship managers on the system need to know that you're listening to them. And they need to know that you regard sales automation as their system.

Beta test budgets

At this point in the implementation process, budgets often start to vanish. "Well, we've spent enough already. Let's try it. Fix anything we need to fix. Then get on with it." Horrible mistake.

Implementing sales automation is a process. If you give up or slack off two-thirds of the way through, you're likely to wind up with nothing. A helpful hint: before you start the entire process, get commitment to provide adequate budget for careful supervision of your beta sites. Recently, I worked on a program where two beta sites got reduced to one because of budget concerns. Then, the program was introduced, but no one from the team ever visited the single beta site after initial training—again, for budget reasons. The beta site changed the program to meet the idiosyncrasies of the region, and the major thrust of the program was lost when the site slid back into expediency mode and started executing the program selectively. The client learned nothing from the test and wasted a very substantial investment in development of program elements representing *the* major payback on the system, elements which are not yet in use.

A very costly error.

PHASE IV

SALES AUTOMATION DEPLOYMENT MAP

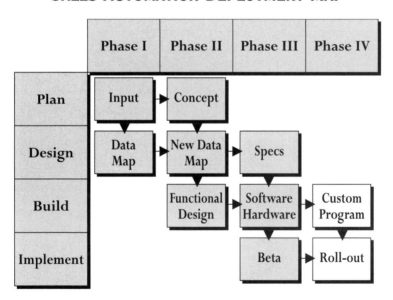

Sales automation is so dynamic that it's fair to call this the beginning of the road, not the end.

I don't know which will relieve you more: that we're at the end of the deployment process or at the end of the book. Hope it's because you're almost through reading, because there really is no end to sales automation deployment. Once you launch your system, you'll probably never stop improving it, as each new wave of technology offers more and more user benefits. It's the stuff that dreams are made of. At least my dreams. But for now, we have to keep grinding it out to get you up and running.

As you may have noticed, I slipped in an additional topic, "training," that's not on the deployment map. Actually, training is an inseparable part of your rollout. But it's so damned important, and it's skimped on so often, that it deserves more than a subhead's worth of discussion.

So, for the last time, let's hit it.

CUSTOM PROGRAMMING

We've already discussed customization in the "Software Selection" section. Now it's time to do it, rather than talk about it. So now you call the software supplier and ask them to do it. Thank you. Next chapter.

I'm serious, at least in part. Whoever developed the software you buy knows their way around it much better than you ever will. That's why it makes sense for them to customize it—at least to the point of laying in the data tables, establishing data relationships, installing wizards to eliminate key strokes, etc. But I'll also state three exceptions to that.

First, if you do succumb and go with a shrink-wrapped program, it's not worth the investment to modify it significantly, especially if the modifications involve tinkering with a flat file database in order to get something out of it. Don't bother customizing. Save your money until you're ready for a more substantial system.

Second, several new programs such as Pivotal Relationship and SalesLogix provide customization tools that let someone who's half a programmer work from outside the system, rather than up to their elbows in code. You may need some "factory" customization, even with these programs, but less than you'll need without these customization tools.

And third, *if* the program is written in Visual Basic (or a variant such as "Access Basic") or in SQL, and *if* you have excellent VB or SQL programmers at your disposal, and *if* the software developer will release enough information to your programmers and otherwise assist them, then you may want to customize yourself. Visual Basic is such a prevalent programming language that you'll probably never be far away from a skilled resource, which is not the case with other languages. And SQL will soon have a similar status, thanks to its growing popularity among Windows NT users.

If you're only developing peripheral application programs that need to link to sales automation, such as a custom quotation program or an on-hand inventory, that's a different story. You're better off building them yourselves or contracting for them locally. No need to pay premium programming rates for generic work. On the other hand, always check with your software vendor to see if they have a similar accessory program on-the-shelf (usually something custom-developed for a prior customer).

But stay away from making heavy-duty modifications to the core program yourself. One of my clients purchased a popular DOS automation program years back, and a VAR started customizing it and customizing it until the program became unrecognizable. It also became unfixable by anyone else, which created an annuity for the VAR doing the customizing. Not

DON'T CONDUCT UNAUTHORIZED EXPERIMENTS ON YOUR SALES AUTOMATION SOFTWARE; IF YOU DO, YOUR SOFTWARE MIGHT PAY YOU BACK.

good. Not for you. And if the truth be told, not good for the VAR long term, either. When time came to replace this chewing-gum-and-bailing-wire system, the VAR got its bell rung, but it wasn't the telephone bell.

Oh, if sales automation software programs could talk about the horrible things we do to them. But they can't—so they burp, hiccup and crash instead.

When you start custom programming, start with the functions designed for relationship managers. It's their system. And if they see you doing stuff for marketing or anyone else who's going to tie in before they've started getting their goodies, it will be one more case of "those closest to the customer matter least." Not the impression you want to give, or the reality you want to deliver.

One little postscript. As alluded to in "Beta Testing," don't try to finish your custom programming all at one time, then unveil it all at one time like a shopping center ribbon-cutting. Phase it in. Let users absorb one element before they start learning the next. Sales automation users aren't computer operators (except for some customer service folks). They need time. They need comfort. So don't overwhelm them. And stay flexible enough to change priorities, or add or subtract custom elements. I've seen too many examples of "this is what they're going to get and they're going to use it whether they like it or not." Fat chance.

TRAINING

By now, you're probably months behind schedule and way over budget. Everyone wants this process over and done with, probably no one more than you (well, not really, but if you act that way you get lots of appreciation and even some sympathy). So the temptation is great to just CUT IT LOOSE. And if your beta tests went well, and any post-test modifications required are complete, you can. If, that is, you can train all users at once. Which you can't, unless you're with a small organization. So you'll probably have to adjust your rollout schedule to your training schedule. And for Pete's sake, don't do it the other way around. Don't adjust your training schedule to your rollout schedule. Otherwise, you may wind up with a "roll off" schedule, where people go on the system the first week and roll off the next.

Preparation

Here's another of the "hot tips" I've tried to drop here and there throughout the book. *Don't wait until two weeks before beta testing to start developing your training program.* While you should wait until after beta-site feedback to finalize your training program—because beta is every bit as much a test of training effectiveness as it is program effectiveness—you should start working on training as soon as you start sales automation deployment, if not before.

Among the key questions you have to ask yourself early on are:

How are you going to change your sales culture, and to a lesser extent your service culture? Remember again, sales automation involves changing human behavior. We're talking about new processes, new approaches to selling, new measurements and goals, and especially new relationships with customers. Sales automation training is not a big "ta da," when the laptops and software show up. If you do it right, the software and laptops are the very tools users have been eagerly awaiting, to start applying the new customer- and information-driven sales and marketing strategy in your organization.

How are you (or your sponsors) going to bring marketing on-board? A marketing-driven company is not a customer-driven company. Sales automation moves you a big step in the direction of customer-driven. For example, sales automation will almost certainly lead to sales customization of most marketing collateral the customer sees. Marketing may provide the raw materials, but sales and service will determine which information goes to whom, and often in what format. That shift in responsibility should trigger a shift in budget. Hard sell to marketing? No question. You might hand out copies of Peppers and Rogers' *Enterprise One to One* or *The One to One Future* to select marketing managers. Then again, you might not. Every organization has to resolve this issue in its own way, but it has to be resolved. Sales automation creates a new connection between customer relationship managers and marketers. It's often not a comfortable connection. Making it comfortable, changing expectations and promoting acceptance of new realities requires an adult dose of adult training—training that has to take place prior to implementation of sales automation.

What's your timing? The entire time you're developing your sales automation system, sales, marketing and field management should be earnestly working to introduce the new customer-centric business strategy that sales automation supports—and winning support for that strategy (unless, of course you're upgrading your sales automation effort rather than starting new). Senior management should be heralding the approach of this "new era" in your organization. Bells should be ringing, whistles blowing, banners streaming and excitement flowing, all long before you load the first laptops with beta software and deliver them to beta sites. All of which, of course, puts pressure on you to deliver the system on schedule.

So here's another hot tip. *From the start, lie about the schedule.* Give yourself an extra three months—even better, four months—beyond the time you believe you can deliver the system if everything goes according to form. For a first-time situation, you should not attempt to deliver a beta system in less than, at minimum, six months; nine months for a complex system. Rollout should not start for another 90 days, except in situations where all the users work under one roof, which may cut that interval down to 30 to 45 days. A replacement system will typically take one-half to two-thirds as long.

What about these "rapid deployment" systems that get you up and going in 90 days, from start to end of process? Great way to sell software. Gets the customer to accept the seller's stuff before needs are known. But you won't know which processes you're automating for a minimum of 60 days after you start, and more likely 90 days. Then you have to match a software system to your processes. What rapid deployment implies, in sales automation terms, is that you're supposed to fit your processes to the software's capabilities, not the other way around. You'll regret doing that, I assure you.

Start training early, but be realistic with future sales automation system users about when they'll see the system.

How computer literate are your sales automation users? It does no good to get users on a computer for the first time months in advance of rollout and for the second time two days before they have to start using the program, but you might think of ways to familiarize them with laptops early on. Maybe doing routine reporting on a simple spreadsheet program or client correspondence on a word processor. The more familiar sales automation users are with operating a computer, with a keyboard, with Windows 95, the easier time they'll have learning your sales automation program. But if a considerable percentage of users won't be computer literate and Windows literate before you and your training staff arrive to teach them sales automation, hold mandatory Windows 95 training for everyone (except the very knowledgeable) as close as possible to the start of sales automation training.

How are you going to train new hires? Turnover is a fact of life. Murphy's law says that you'll have several new hires at every site the week after sales automation training. So what do you do? You need to develop two resources: First, you'll need a complete training manual plus (hopefully) a CD-ROM training program that new hires can self-administer. Second, at each field location you'll need a designated trainer who will coach and support new hires (as well as existing staff). Is this a substantial overhead expense? You betcha. But you can "pay it now," or "pay it later" in lost productivity and lost information. Paying it now is much less expensive.

How will you train the trainers? Don't wait to train your field trainers until you and your entourage arrive on-site. Bring them in to corporate HQ in advance. Thoroughly teach them the program (the best time is when you're starting to beta test). Involve them in the updating and fixing that comes out of beta. Let your trainers become beta test sites themselves. Even consider giving one or two sales and service people beta programs to run unsupervised in their regions, with the agreement that they'll use the system and report back the successes and problems.

> **TRAIN YOUR FIELD TRAINERS BEFORE BEGINNING ON-SITE SESSIONS.**

Then, when you arrive, you have on-site help. New program users find it greatly comforting to have people whom they know and who can already use the program present during training. When it comes to computers, few of us like to rely solely on ourselves.

What should you ask of your software supplier? As much as you want to pay for, but not more than they're capable of providing.

Sales automation developers are not trainers. Neither are most sales automation salespeople. Training is a profession unto itself.

Some software companies have full-time trainers on staff. But I strongly recommend that you use them primarily to train your trainers, both HQ and field types.

What should you ask of internal training resources? Fortunately, if you're with a larger organization you may have training professionals on staff. Also fortunately, most training professionals are highly computer literate. Enlist them. Have them learn the system. Ask them for suggestions. Make them your partners. Marry them. Whatever. Get them on your team from the beginning, and make them important team members.

When you plan training, rely on your internal training resources to map out the process and plan the specifics. Then, when training time arrives, support your trainers in every session with technical experts in the product. For the first few sessions, you might want a technical (not sales) representative from the software company present. After you or your staff masters the technical responses to common questions, you should be able to handle things yourself. And here's another tip. When the software representative isn't present, especially in early the sessions, *arrange a conference call with a technician in the middle or at the end of each training day.* Just make sure they have an exact copy of your program, including any sample databases you're using, loaded and ready to use.

What if you're with a smaller organization without adequate, internal training resources? Hire an experienced trainer from the outside. Then use them as you would an internal resource. Sure it's expensive, but so is having your project fail. Don't skimp here.

Execution

We've talked about most training particulars already, but I want to underscore one point. *Make a big deal out of it.* Sales automation is the start of a new and exciting phase in the life of a business, and training is the moment of birth. When sales automation users head out the training room door, with their laptops and their software and their customer and prospect database already loaded, it's a beginning and it should feel that way. Don't let training end late on a Friday afternoon, with everyone itching to leave a session that threatens never to end but has lost so much focus and momentum that it can barely crawl to the finish line. Sales automation training should be a celebration, not some administrative duty tucked into whatever someone considers the least productive time period.

REPORT THE SUCCESSES OF YOUR SALES AUTOMATION PROGRAM TO MOTIVATE USERS.

Enjoy it! And make sure everyone leaves excited and ready to meet and enjoy this new challenge.

And then reinforce it. Start a sales automation newsletter to report the triumphs and deal with the problems honestly and openly. Set up call-in conferences for groups of system users to share issues and opportunities. Have user incentive programs prepared and ready to go, so users are motivated to take the simple steps, like acquiring and entering key information from customers, by unexpectedly rewarding some that do.

Remember that training is much more than telling people what you want them to do. It's motivating them to do it. Rewarding them when they do. And constantly reinforcing desired behaviors. Training starts early—then lasts as long as sales automation itself.

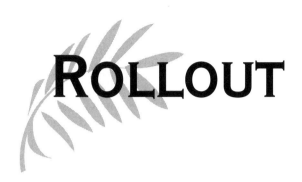

ROLLOUT

Hey, what's left to do? Before we started, you probably would have named "software selection" and "rollout" as the two high points of deploying sales automation. But it turns out, they're both sort of duds. All the real work is done before you got there. All that's left now is to coordinate shipment of hardware and software, and schedule and administer training. Pretty dull stuff, after all the fun you've had.

Of course, there will be problems to solve, glitches to fix, tempers to soothe and gratification from starting to see positive changes in behaviors and process measurements. Hopefully, too, pats on the back for doing a good job, perhaps a well-deserved promotion, perhaps a very well-deserved rest.

The training process, including reinforcement, must continue. But even that's going to feel a little anti-climactic.

So you did it. You pulled it off. Congratulations. What's next? How can it be as exciting as sales automation?

Wait a minute. You're not done. You've barely begun. When I said "rollout," you probably thought I meant rolling out sales automation to sales and service users. You were only half right.

I also meant rolling out sales automation internally, to marketing, accounting, logistics, wherever customer information is
present. And then rolling out each new development phase
(remember, we weren't going to overwhelm users by launching
the entire system in one fell swoop). It's the rollout from sales
automation to enterprise sales automation that comes next.
And if you think your first set of challenges were bracing, wait
until you see the opportunity ahead of you now.

But that's another assignment, another process, another
book. Time for a vacation. From reading. From writing. From
thinking. But not for long. This stuff is too much fun to leave
alone for very long. I know it's that way for me. I suspect it will
be that way for you, too, once you get a real taste of it. If you
like being at the center of the action, the action doesn't get
much better than this.

SIDEBARS

I wanted an opportunity to share with you stuff that's been floating around in my head while I've been writing that didn't really fit in the text, hence, these "sidebars." Ranging from a tongue-in-cheek Ten Commandments (of Sales Automation) to some depressing thoughts about ageist sales automation implementation practices, each sidebar presents information that you may want to share with others in your organization as you contemplate, and I hope implement, sales automation.

Thanks for reading, and I hope that I've helped you prepare for the challenges of sales automation.

THE TEN COMMANDMENTS (OF SALES AUTOMATION)

1. Thou shall respect the full magnitude of sales automation and not act hastily about it.

2. Thou shall respect the primacy of relationships with customers.

3. Thou shall honor those closest to customers, for they are feeding you.

4. Thou shall endeavor to empower relationship managers, not enslave them.

5. Thou shall place the needs of relationship managers first and corporate needs second.

6. Thou shall strive to manage as much customer information as possible at points of customer contact.

7. Thou shall always remember that sales automation collects information from customers, rather than delivering information to sales.

8. Thou shall understand that sales sells by process or by accident, and accidents don't happen often enough.

9. Though shall dedicate your sales automation efforts to improving process, not increasing control.

10. Thou shall not buy software until you know what the hell you're doing.

Silence From Above

In most sales automation implementations, the most important player is the CEO. That's not a mantle most chief executives want to accept. "Not strategic enough to warrant my time." "That's a middle management job." "My managers need to work things out themselves, that's what we pay them for." Wrong. Wrong. Wrong.

1. *Sales automation is the first step in the process of reorienting a business around its customers.* If it fails, and 60% to 70% of sales automation initiatives do fail, so does the effort to become a customer-focused business. It doesn't get much more strategically focused than that.

2. *Putting middle management in sole charge of sales automation increases the chances of failure from 60% or 70% to 100%.* To repeat the saying of my organizational development colleague, Ralph Jacobson, "Change the information flow and you change the company." Sales automation changes information flow dramatically, and it changes the company dramatically. Middle managers aren't empowered to change companies.

3. *Sales automation breaks down management silos.* Asking senior executives to give up departmental or divisional authority, even subordinate themselves to other executives, is serious stuff. Smart CEOs don't expect their senior managers to roll over and "take one for the Gipper." The smart ones know they need to proactively design a new, customer-centered organization and take the lead in implementing that new organization.

Part and parcel of a CEO's (or a comparable senior executive's) washing their hands of sales automation is the train wreck that occurs at the middle management level, with the poor middle manager who gets run over while trying to implement sales automation. Every consultant I know in the business has seen this happen, often multiple times. It makes us sick to our stomachs, and it leaves us wanting to throttle those at the helm who let it happen.

Here's what goes down. A middle manager gets assigned to implement sales automation. If the person is lucky, he or she has a reasonably strong sponsor. They stroke, soothe, cajole, jawbone and finesse their way through all of the normal hurdles that sales automation implementers face. Finally, they're ready to go—to beta, to buying hardware and software, to announcing the new enterprise sales automation system to the enterprise, whatever. But they're about to do something too visible and too significant for a middle manager to get credit for in their corporate environment.

So with the blessing of the CEO, or whomever, in sashay nefarious corporate climbers with visions of career advancement dancing in their heads. And they take over the project in a very paternalistic way. "Nice job so far, but I'd better finish this for you." Boy, do they finish it.

First, the whole focus of the system starts changing, from benefiting the customer and relationship managers to benefiting corporate management. Next, you start hearing talk like, "They'll use the system [sales automation] because we'll tell them to use it." Then the corporate climbers convert sales automation into a flashy Internet sideshow that feeds nothing but egos. Meanwhile, some poor middle manager gets chewed up and spit out on the corporate dung heap.

You can blame the interlopers, who surely deserve all of the blame you can heap on them. But they could only trash the project because somebody let them. Their CEOs. Their sponsors. A bunch of folks who were supposed to be looking out for the company.

If you want a second opinion on this, read "An Open Letter to the CEO," which concludes Don Peppers and Martha Rogers' *Enterprise One To One.** The tone may be more forgiving than mine, but the message is the same. We've all been there. Seen that. Fought that. And we feel for the innocent and loyal employees who get used. And we recognize the damage that your silence and complicity does to your organizations.

You, CEO, cannot afford to be silent.

---

* Don Peppers and Martha Rogers, Enterprise One To One, (New York: Doubleday, 1997).

AGEISM

I treat my clients with great respect, or at least try to. After all, they're my customers. They're paying me. And while they deserve my honest and objective thinking, they deserve that delivered in a reasoned and professional manner.

But when I hear someone say, "It's a good opportunity to 'lose' some of our older folks," or "The old guys will never learn to run computers," or similar stuff, I get my dander up. Sales automation is no excuse for discriminatory employment practices, intentional or otherwise.

The conscious stuff is actually easy to deal with. I won't work with a client who intentionally practices ageism. I can't change a discriminatory mindset, and I won't stick around to try.

But the unconscious stuff is another matter. Sales automation generates a very substantial amount of unintentional ageism. Here's how it happens.

You just "know" that so-and-so is totally averse to using a computer, any kind of computer, for any purpose. You have a legitimate need to require your relationship managers to work on computer with your sales automation system. You know so-and-so won't do it, so you figure you'll have to "lose" them.

But wait a minute. *Why* won't this person use a computer? Why will they hold out, at the risk of losing their job?

Usually because they're intimidated. They lack confidence that they can learn to use one. They feel inferior to younger employees who can't yet carry their briefcase in terms of forging and maintaining customer relationships, but who are very facile "on the box." They often feel less valued than younger employees, who have contributed much less to the organization than they have. And they resent having to deal with these feelings after years of good service to the organization.

What comes across as belligerence and obstinacy is usually fear of failure and resentment over how they're being treated on this issue.

So, do you "lose" them anyway. And what do you "lose" if you do. You lose a ton of relationship management savvy, a commodity that's in very short supply these days, with the negative baggage that being in sales has acquired. You also may lose customers, a commodity that's in even shorter supply. You lose leadership and mentoring resources that are hard, if not impossible, to replace.

Now let's talk about the "cost" of keeping these resources: A confidential conversation to let them know that, although you understand their reluctance to use a computer, you need their leadership in implementing sales automation, so you're going to help them get acclimated. A special class in running a computer; followed by another in Windows 95; both exclusively for non-computer users, preferably at an off-site location and led by an outside trainer who understands that the primary goal is having fun and creating a comfort level. A little patience and support, a little extra training, lots of encouragement and understanding that becoming a computer user at an older age involves a range of difficult feelings.

A very small price to pay to keep these resources. If you want to keep them, you usually can. Not always, just as you can't always turn around a difficult situation with a younger employee. But most of the time.

Please recognize that you are asking more of older employees than their younger counterparts when you ask them to adopt sales automation and work on computer. You'll have to work harder with them to help them through the transition. But what you get back is repayment many times over your efforts. If you sense anywhere in your organization sentiments that sales automation means ditching the "old folks," please try to turn that around.

Quo Vadis, It?

Thought it might be appropriate to use a Latin title for a subject that's Greek to most of us.

Whither are you going, IT?

Not back to where you came from before sales automation and before customer knowledge management, that's for sure.

Today's corporate information systems are still internally focused and quantitatively based. They're centered around internal operations such as finance, manufacturing, inventory control, payroll, logistics and the like, and they rely almost exclusively on "hard," quantitative data. Even though American business traditionally has been internally focused, the necessity to have customers in the business loop puts our internally-focused information systems at odds with our information needs today—even before the advent of fundamental cultural changes that will redirect corporate focus toward customers.

Every time I map a client's current data flow, I see the conflict between system design and customer information needs. The conflict often manifests itself in a tortuous routing of data that is required for IT to maintain control; in the unnecessary data movement necessitated by outmoded concepts, such as "no data is safe unless it's in the central data vault;" in the blind allegiance to quantitative data, without regard for how misinforming "what" data can be when unaccompanied by "why" knowledge.

Fortunately, our business culture is gradually changing its orientation and becoming customer rather than internally focused. That can't help but have a dramatic effect on corporate information systems and the people who design, build and operate them.

Want proof?

Try mapping out your customer data flow as it currently exists, from sales to shipping, service to manufacturing, accounting to human resources to inventory management...everywhere there's an information system. You'll see information management "islands" in each area. A few will have strong bridges between them. More will have rickety bridges between them. Even more will have no bridges. And a few will be surrounded by moats filled with hungry crocodilians.

Then play "what if" and re-map customer data flow to best serve customers, not back-office operatives. Eliminate all the islands (damn the crocodiles, full speed ahead!). Design a single, integral customer record that everyone in the enterprise shares. Consider all customer-related information (including inventory and manufacturing information that affects customer orders) as tools to provide value to customers first, and then accommodate internal functional needs second.

Astonishing things happen when you re-route data around the customer. You'll see how information systems can become simpler and more manageable. System workloads can decrease. Human workloads can decrease. And you realize how much, even today, information systems are out of sync with business processes, compromising systems and processes both.

Once you've seen this, you can't go back. But where will you go instead?

CUSTOMER KNOWLEDGE MANAGEMENT

Knowledge management is among the hottest information technology topics—in research, engineering, manufacturing and other corporate areas. But not yet in sales and marketing.

Why not? For one thing, sales and marketing sit at the end of the technology line. At least they have. They've been taken care of after everyone else's needs have been met once, twice, maybe three times. And frankly, that's been fine with sales and marketing, where the "right brain" still rules.

Also, we mistakenly identify customer marketing, relationship marketing, one-to-one marketing, whatever…as "database marketing." And database marketing is 100% quantitative, as are its supporting data warehouses, both relying entirely on "what" data.

But sales automation is equal parts "why" knowledge of customers and "what" data about customers and their past behavior. Funny. The new breed of knowledge management systems emerging outside of sales and marketing have that same balance between "why" knowledge and "what" data.

I see a marriage coming. Not so much a marriage of information technology, although that will occur, but a marriage between perspectives from two ends of the enterprise. Both appreciate the vital importance of soft information about hunches, experiences, issues, observations and facts that don't reduce down to numbers.

That's why I believe we're going to be talking about "customer knowledge management" and "customer knowledgeware" and "customer knowledge systems" in the near future. That's why we're going to see our customer knowledge systems meet operations knowledge systems midway within the enterprise. And then they're going to shake hands and start jabbering back and forth. Happy little systems, now that they've each found a mate.

Think I'm overreaching a bit? I don't. In fact, I'm thinking back to the 1980s when I started describing what my then "advertising" agency did as "micromarketing." To the dismay of even my own staff. "No one knows what that is." "Hell, we don't know what that is." And in my own, inarticulate way, I couldn't explain it very well—at least not in a way that stuck for more than the length of an encounter or a workshop or a journal article.

But I could feel this sea change in marketing and sales and customer service and marketing communication coming. Like arthritic hands predicting the weather. And it finally came. Only about five years after I though it would.

Now everyone knows what micromarketing is. It's what we have to do now that mass marketing is losing its steam. It's seeing markets as heterogeneous, rather than homogenous. It's figuring out what makes customers different, rather than searching for what they have in common. You know. The stuff that sales automation is made of.

I was right once. I'm even more convinced that my "hands" are reading the wind and weather shift correctly this time. Within the next several years, I believe, a wave of knowledge-based thinking and working is going to break over the boundaries that separate sales from marketing from service, and all three from operations. Lots of corporate silos will fall, although only after being battered by a good many waves. Lots of strange bedfellows will result. And the transition from information to knowledge will only fuel the transition from internally-focused organizations to customer-focused organizations. It has to, because the transition from "information about" to "knowledge of" customers will give us the power to forge customer relationships like we've never experienced before.

Trust me. Just cut me five years slack on the timing.

Glossary of Acronyms and Other Potentially Befuddling Terms

Back office. Functions such as manufacturing, finance and accounting, human resources, logistics that have but incidental contact with customers.

CIM. Customer information management, usually provided by a CIS (see below).

CIS. Customer information system, typically an extension of a back office system.

Client-server. A computer network system that includes both a central computer (server) and individual PCs (clients). Processing work is split between server and clients, making for a much more efficient use of resources than with a mainframe/dumb terminal system or a LAN that shares data but does all processing on PCs.

Customer data warehouse. Giant vat into which raw customer data is poured, occasionally stirred, then theoretically tapped by whomever needs it. Customer data warehouses are focused on quantitative information, and therefore offer much less than a complete picture of customers and their actions.

DDE. Stands for dynamic data exchange, which is the automated transfer of data from one software program to another. Gradually being replaced by OLE automation (see below).

Enterprise sales automation. Systematic customer information management that starts at the point of customer contact, then works back into the back room.

Flat file. Old-style database that stores all information in one table or folder. Still used for high-speed, high-volume processing of simple sets of data.

Front office. Functions such as sales, customer service and marketing focused on customers.

GCM. Group contact management software designed for operation on both networks and free-standing computers. GCMs allow work groups to share customer information, but they typically lack relational databases (see below) and they have limited capabilities for integrating with back office functions. Not robust enough for most sales automation application.

HLTV. High lifetime value, usually applied to good customers retained over time.

ICM. Individual contact management software designed for independent operation by the user. Inadequate for sales automation purposes.

IT. The information technology department within an organization.

LAN. Technically, any network of computers in one locale; but in application, a network in one locale that holds data in a central computer but relies on individual PCs to do all the processing.

LAN-sync. Synchronizing data held on laptops to a local, "master" database; then, synchronizing these local databases to a central, corporate database.

Marketing database. Typically a direct marketing database that supports direct mail and telemarketing communication. Plays limited support role in sales automation.

MDS. Management decision system, which would be more properly called a management data system. Lots of data, little information; thus often a terrible source of misinformation.

ODBC. Open database connectivity—a feature incorporated into many Windows-based programs that allows them to access network databases.

OLE. automation Automated object linking and embedding that allows one database to populate another. Linking provides automated updating across databases.

Open architecture. Design that permits attachment of additional components. Originally used only for hardware, but now often applied to software.

Operating system. The basic set of instructions that govern how a computer relates to hardware components such as disk drives, monitors, printers, modems and the like. Most software is written to work in conjunction with one specific operating system or several closely related systems (such as Windows 3.1 and Windows 95).

PDA. Hand-held electronic calender/phone book such as 3Com's® Palm Pilot. HHC (hand held computers is another acronym for these little guys).

PIM. Personal information management software. Like an ICM, but less.

Relational database. Database that stores related information in separate tables. Allows for cross-referencing data to establish data relationships. A relational database provides powerful analysis capabilities that flat files don't.

Remote data syncronization. Swapping data between non-networked computers in order to keep everyone running on the same data.

RM. Relationship management software systems which manage both customer information and sales and marketing processes; the "real deal" as far as sales automation is concerned.

Sales automation. Systematic management of customer information and customer-related activities, especially among sales, service and marketing.

SFA. Sales force automation, which sales automation used to be called when it only involved field salespeople.

SQL. A powerful language for writing database queries in a client-server network environment. SQL is becoming a standard for database developers. SQL is an abbreviation for "sequel," not for "structured query language" as commonly believed.

Sequel Server. A complete, client-server database built around the SQL language; becoming a standard in the sales automation business.

TOC. Theory of constraints, or TOC, is an analysis approach, usually applied to manufacturing. TOC identifies process bottlenecks that limit down-line work or cause upstream buildups. Eliminating these bottlenecks in marketing and sales processes can create huge cost-savings and revenue increases. The process analysis required to design sales automation systems often identifies these bottlenecks, and sales automation measurements help control them.

UNIX®. A multiuser operating system designed for use on minicomputers. Because there are few sales automation software applications written for UNIX, attempting to develop sales automation on a UNIX platform is almost always a lost cause. As minicomputers are replaced by more and more powerful PCs, UNIX is often replaced by Windows operating systems.

VAR. Value-added reseller that theoretically adds value to products and systems before selling them to end-users. While many information systems VARs do add substantial value through systems integration or specialized software or knowledgeable installation and configuration, many others, especially in sales automation, add nothing but markup.

WAN. A network of remote computers that all tie directly to a central, corporate database.

WAN-SYNC. Synchronizing directly with a central, corporate database.

"What" data. Quantitative data (expressed in numerical format).

"Why" data. Qualitative data (expressed in text format).

BIOGRAPHY

Dick Lee is founder and principal of the St. Paul, Minnesota-based consulting group, High-Yield Marketing (HYM). HYM helps clients develop and accomplish relationship marketing strategies through specialized planning techniques; construction of relationship marketing tools (such as sales automation and enterprise customer information systems); and utilization of these tools. Prior to forming HYM in 1994, Dick was co-founder and president of Lee & Riley, perhaps the first "micromarketing agency" and a laboratory for testing and introducing many customer- and information-driven communication methods in common use today.

Over his marketing career, Dick's clients have included 3M Company, AMR (American Airlines), American Express, Fidelity Investments, General Mills, Microsoft and Pitney-Bowes. However, he has a soft spot for middle market and even small clients, about which he says, "Less politics means more progress."

Dick's seminal marketing work has been covered by diverse media, including The Wall Street Journal, AdWeek, Direct Marketing News, Potentials in Marketing and National Public Radio's MarketPlace. Dick holds a BA from Reed College, Portland, Oregon, and an MBA from Suffolk University, Boston. Before deciding to share his professional experiences through writing, he taught both direct marketing and micromarketing at the Graduate School of Business, University of St. Thomas, Minneapolis. While Dick has written for numerous professional journals, this is his first book.